© Healthful Dog 2017

CW00435523

Contents

From the Editor

Hello Readers.

Welcome to our Autumn edition of Healthful Dog Journal. You will fin magazine jam packed with really informative articles, ranging from information about the food our beloved dog's and cats eat to information on kind and gentle dog grooming, and how to help our dog's deal with the noise of fireworks. Plus lots of useful information about various physical therapies to help with pain and discomfort.

If you have an interest in all things holistic when it comes to helping your dogs, you will find it in this journal. It is well worth every penny in my humble opinion. Yes, I know I would say that, I am the Editor after all.

However, I am passionate about helping animals holistically whenever possible, whether it is to do with their food, their health or their behaviour, all of which are linked.

Would you do me a favour please? If you enjoy reading this journal, don't keep it to yourself. Tell your friends about it, post about it on the internet, help us spread the word to make our dogs lives so much healthier. Thank you.

Happy reading folks.

See you next time.

Elaine Downs

N.B. Natural products and holistic services should not be considered a substitute for veterinary treatment. If you suspect your animal is ill, please take them to your nearest veterinary surgeon as soon as possible.

HEALTHFUL DOG
www.HealthfulDog.co.uk

The UKs No 1 Holistic Pet Health Magazine

Copyright © Healthful 2011 - 2017

Editor: Elaine Downs   Photo Editor: John Fieldsend   Advertising Manager: Nick Harding

 Facebook.com/HealthfulDog
Plus.google.com/+HealthfulUKDogs
www.youtube.com/c/HealthfulUKDogs

 twitter.com/HealthfulDog
healthfuldog.podbean.com

pinterest.com/healthfuldog
instagram.com/healthful_dog
vimeo.com/healthfuldog

Bardic the Newshound

Long Living Pets Research is a non-profit trying to help pets to be healthier. They currently have 3 research projects going on

1 - The Odin Project (feeding raw)
2 - Cancer Prevention (using a natural protocol)
3 - Cancer Help (using a natural protocol)
You can join these research projects for FREE online.

https://longlivingpets.com/the-research-projects

Canine First Aid with Rachel Bean RVN Saturday 3rd September CentreBarks Doggie DayCare, Gallowfields Ind Est, DL10 £45 per person Centrebarksyorkshire.co.uk	**How Animal Healing Can Transform Your Relationship with your Pet** Wednesday 13th September Trying Holistics, Mrs Howard Hall, SG6 1NX £12 TryingHolistics.com
Canine 5 Elements Massage Training Saturday 16th—Sunday 17th September The School of Fine Tuning, Southbourne BH6 £165 Annamal.co.uk/classes.html	**Raw Diet & Vaccines Seminar** Nick Thompson Saturday 23rd September Canine Acadamy, Tollerton Lane, Nottingham £69 per person denise@cadelac.co.uk
Canine Firework Support Workshop Saturday 30th September Hartsop Farm, Witney Road, Finstock, Oxon £65 per person Myanimalmatters.co.uk	**Ian Dunbar 4 day dog training seminar** Tues 10th—Fri 13th October Stoneleigh Park, Coventry £85 https://www.dog-and-bone.co.uk/seminars
HELP! My Dog's Scared of Fireworks Toni Shelbourne Saturday 14th October East Farleigh WI Hall, Maidstone £15—£60 Tonishelbourne.co.uk	**Building Drive & Motivation for All Dog Sports** Denise Fenzi 23rd-24th November - Gloucester 27th-28th November - Doncaster £139 https://www.dog-and-bone.co.uk/seminars

Book Review
The Power of Bailey, Bach & Verbeia Essences for Animals

By Caroline Thomas

Animals suffer from emotional stress just like humans, which the Bailey, Bach and Verbeia Essences are able to help.

The modern world that our animals live in is far removed from their evolutionary path and adds anxiety to their daily lives. In the wild, horses would explore their large environment in herds and dogs would live in packs.

The Bailey, Bach and Verbeia Essences are here to bring back the utopia of that time, by allowing animals to live out their lives in peace. The Flower Essences are made with only the energy of the flowers so they can be taken alongside other medications; they are also 100% safe. The Essences help to alleviate, fear, grief, anxiety, separation anxiety, excessive grooming and so much more.

Caroline is an Animal Holistic Therapist and writer. She has been using Flower Essences with Animals for over fourteen years and has helped many animals with complex emotional issues. She has clients all over the world who have benefited from the magic of these Essences. Caroline teaches Holistic Therapies for Animals online to Practitioner level and is also very passionate about working with Rescued Animals.

This book is filled with information about flower essences and has new discoveries about how flower essences work with animals.

Often, books of this nature are very soft and don't focus on the scientific and written evidence for such complementary medicines.
The book also acts as a compendium, being able to reference each individual flower and essence.

http://www.emotionalhealing4animals.co.uk/

Flexibility: The bane and the benefit of prey model raw feeding your cat.

Tracy Dion

CatCentric

It's a given that in today's society, most of us are crazy busy. We've got boyfriends/girlfriends or husbands/wives, kids, friends, family, jobs and all the ups and downs of daily life. It's no wonder the convenience of spending all of two minutes to grab a bag or a can and dump the contents into a pet's bowl is the driving force behind the near-universal popularity of processed diets.

Time, however, has begun to show us how harmful those diets actually are, and as growing numbers of pet parents take to the internet in search of healthier options – ones that don't provoke allergies, obesity, diabetes, kidney disease and more – an understanding of the incredibly amazing benefits of providing our cats with wholesome, raw, species-appropriate food is spreading.

Unfortunately, even as more pet parents realize how profoundly the health of their beloved furchildren has been impacted by those convenient but insanely over-processed products, the pressures of their busy lives continue unabated. Because the pet food industry lacks any desire to research balanced fresh raw diets – understandably so – and veterinarians seldom have the resources to research on their own and so lean on those self-same PFI representatives for nutritional input, pet parents are left to fend for themselves as they attempt to improve their pets' diets. Finding the time to research all the many raw feeding options and weigh the differing opinions can sometimes be overwhelming, and some become so discouraged they reluctantly turn back to commercially processed foods.

Many cat owners find CatCentric before they reach that point, and I receive emails every week asking for a simple, straight-forward no-need-to-think-about-it raw feeding recipe. If you're contemplating a ground diet, no problem, I can refer you to several well-researched and tested recipes (although I don't, as a general rule, recommend ground as a long-term diet option). If, however, you're looking for a prey model raw (PMR) – or "frankenprey" – menu or recipe... well, nothing would make me happier than to be able to satisfy your requests, but it's just not possible to offer anything more than examples. (Like this one.)

PMR is a concept. After you understand the 83/7/5/5 guideline (that's 83% meat, fat, skin, sinew, connective tissue and heart, 7% edible bone, 5% liver, and 5% other secreting organ) and establish the percentages for your particular cats (see A Frank-enprey / Whole Prey Feeding Guide for details), everything about the PMR methodology is customizable to your circumstances – budget, resources, personal choices, etc. – and the only person who has full access to those logistics is you. I can help you understand the percentages and create a schedule, but the actual menu choices will have to be researched and chosen by you.

Best Food Article
2016

Coupled with the usually comparatively lower cost, this flexibility is one of the prime benefits for pet owners who wish to feed their cats a raw diet. Can't get beef where you are, but kangaroo is popular? No problem, you can incorporate kangaroo into a PMR diet. Feel strongly against supporting factory farming practices and prefer to buy local, naturally raised meat? It's totally fine to substitute one for the other. Your kitty has been diagnosed with chronic kidney disease and needs a low phosphorus diet? PMR can easily be tweaked to adjust to many specialized dietary needs, including a low phosphorus diet that supports kidney health.

Not only can a PMR diet can be modified to fit just about any set of circumstances, it is, in fact, inherently defined by the special, unique set of circumstances personal to every family. That it can be customized so specifically makes it the perfect choice for cat owners wishing to offer their furry little friends one of the healthiest diet options available.

Just don't ask me to send you the "recipe".

www.CatCentric.org

CatCentric

Better lives through better care!

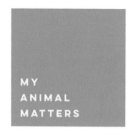

MY
ANIMAL
MATTERS

TESTED BY ANIMALS

Dog with spinal condition given new lease of life

Written by Robyn of Equenergy

I've recently been working with a canine client, Willow, who has been experiencing loss of strength and sensitivity in her hind legs. The vet diagnosed a lesion, within her spinal canal but outside of the spinal cord, causing compression at the T7 vertebra and resulting in weakness and loss of sensation.

A truly holistic approach

In this article I'll describe how Willow's owner, another therapist and I have worked together to support Willow and I'll also share how she's doing now.

I began by taking a history of Willow's condition and reading the vet report. Having done a basic META-Health analysis I felt that, in addition to the Reiki that I would be offering, she would benefit from a Botanical self-healing session and so I recommended Rachel Windsor-Knott of My Animal Matters particularly as she now offers consultations via Skype.

Willow's owner went ahead with this straight away, contacting Rachel, filling in the consultation form and booking in a session, which I was also able to attend.

Empowering Willow with a voice and a choice

Rachel had put together a box of oil and herb samples that, having read the vet report and Willow's information, she thought Willow might find helpful. She started by asking the owner to offer the Ginger essential oil (warming, soothing and analgesic). Willow sniffed and accepted the oil - a gentle 'yes'.

Rachel then moved on to Peppermint and Birch (on cloths) both of which Willow sniffed, seeming to favour the Peppermint.

Peppermint is an anti-inflammatory, a digestive stimulant - often selected by animals taking strong painkillers - and is often selected in cases of nerve damage as it is clarifying and stimulating. Birch is often selected by animals with inflammatory pain, muscular aches and trapped nerves.

Having offered some essential oils, we then moved on to the 2 macerates that Rachel had thought would help Willow: Comfrey and Arnica.
Willow devoured these, lapping up all that Rachel had sent.
Comfrey - also known as 'knit bone' - is often selected by animals with fractures and with soft tissue damage.
It can soothe inflammation of the stomach, too, so may be helpful in easing the side effects of pain killing medication. Arnica is often selected by animals with bruising, muscular injury and inflammatory pain. It is also an immune system stimulant.

Rachel then suggested offering the Rose and Valerian Root hydrosols. Willow licked and chewed at the bottles so her owner poured some out and again she lapped these up and wanted more. She seemed to have a slight preference for the Rose hydrosol.

Rose is often selected in cases of anger and resentment, hormone balancing, feelings of rejection and emotional wounds, trauma and depression.
Valerian root is a muscle relaxant and sedative which is extremely popular in cases of anxious behaviours.

We then moved on to Marjoram Sweet essential oil.

This was on a cloth and again Willow showed interest. Her energy came up and she appeared quite playful.

She approached her owner which made Rachel think she might want to have the oil applied. Rachel gave instructions for Willow's owner to rub the cloth on her hands and offer these to Willow. Willow presented her chest to her owner so she gently rubbed her hands first on Willow's chest, then her neck and shoulders and on down to her back.

Willow then turned round and presented her rump and back for the oil to be applied there too! This oil is an antispasmodic and is often selected where there is stiffness in the muscles. It is also very comforting in cases of grief.

Lastly there was a cloth with Violet Leaf absolute on it. Willow showed great interest in this, chewing at the cloth. This oil is very supportive when there is anticipation of pain. It is comforting to the heart and helps those of a nervous disposition.

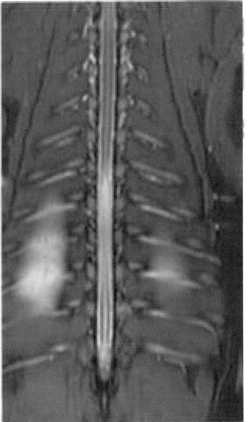

Having offered all of the remedies that Rachel had sent - of which Willow accepted every single one - we then put each remedy on the floor and watched to see what she would do.
She lay down with her jaw parallel to the Peppermint oil.

As Willow was lying there she began to twitch gently, as if she was dreaming, and she did appear to be asleep. During the session she had also shown blinks, yawns, licking, chewing and stretches as she worked with the oils, processing and releasing.

Rachel recommended continuing to offer this selection to Willow, particularly the Peppermint, Marjoram Sweet and Violet Leaf oils, the Comfrey and Arnica macerates and the Rose water.

She also suggested adding rice bran oil and / or coconut oil to Willow's diet (separately from her food bowl so she could self-dose) to ensure that when she chooses the macerates this is done solely for the herb content rather than the fat.

Fat is essential for nerves so she might be choosing these remedies for this as well, particularly as she's on a dry food diet which can result in low levels of healthy fats.
Coconut oil is also antibacterial, antifungal and antiviral so helps with infections. The vet had said that this is a possible cause for the lesion in Willow's spine so this oil might be beneficial in this way too. It is also good for the skin and coat, and supports the thyroid.

A dramatic improvement after one session

The day after the session Willow's owner posted this message:

"Hey! Just wanted to say - Wow!! Willow's legs have improved dramatically! After only one session! So I'm very hopeful and can't wait to continue on with it.

Less collapsing ... she also seems more relaxed and affectionate and her muscles are softer. She is always tense and alert being the alpha dog and protects the house... this morning seems a bit tense/back to normal but no collapsing yet, plus she told us she needed to go outside for a poo (she has been having a lot of accidents so we have to make sure she goes out regularly) so she is definitely feeling her back end and legs again.

Thanks again!"

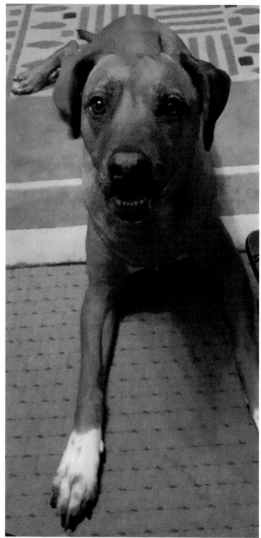

Rachel also recommended that Willow's owner offer her Coconut oil in addition to the remedies to make sure that she was choosing the macerates for their herb content, rather than for fats. Willow proved to be very keen on this and her owner realised that it has also been helping her skin. Willow had had a tendency to lick at her paws causing redness and broken skin but this has now cleared up.

Rachel added Spirulina to Willow's selection of remedies. This is helpful in cases of anxious behaviours and joint problems. It is de-toxifying and helps to stimulate the immune system. It's also a great supplement for senior dogs or those who are a little run-down as it is rich in protein and nutrients. Willow proved to be very fond of this too!

Much more relaxed and softer...

Following the initial session, Willow's owner continued to offer the remedies, particularly the Peppermint, Marjoram Sweet and Violet Leaf oils, the Comfrey and Arnica macerates and the Rose wa-ter. To these she then added the Coconut Oil and Spirulina. She shared this message with us when her box of remedies arrived:

"Willow was so excited when your parcel arrived and was ripping off the bubble wrap with me! She's loving the arnica, comfrey, violet leaf (rubs on side of head with it and mouthing/chewing the cloth) and marjoram on her back, more than the others... She is much more relaxed and softer..."

Rachel had included small sachets of Devil's Claw and Barley Grass which Willow took for a few days.
Devils Claw is selected where there is arthritis, inflammatory pain and musculoskeletal issues. Barley Grass supports animals with anxious and hyperactive behaviours and those with skin condi-tions. It is rich in nutrients, particularly magnesium. Her owner then sent us this message:

"Not keen on devils claw today so offered barley wheat grass ... then offered spirulina... Lucky I put a towel down, specks of green everywhere! ... Still wanting marjoram on her back and generally sleeps with either violet leaf/peppermint.
Willow is twitching now, she hasn't done that for a while."

Throughout this whole process I was also offering Reiki to Willow to help her body enter into it's Rest and Re-pair mode.
She can tend to be an anxious dog who is always on the alert so the Reiki helped her to relax so that her body could heal and so that the oils and other remedies could work effectively. Several of the remedies she chose were also supporting her on this emotional level.

"Willow now almost looks normal when she walks"

In our fifth session, Willow's owner said that had she not seen it for herself she would not have believed the change in her dog over the last month.! From having been very wobbly on her back legs and walking with a rather odd, wide-legged gait, scuffing her toes, Willow now almost looks normal when she walks.
She had lost some muscle tone but is slowly building this up again as she regains strength and feeling.
She now knows when she needs to go outside for toileting and so there have been no further accidents in the house.
Her owner is overjoyed!
When she'd first been given the diagnosis from the vet she had thought she might soon have to say goodbye to her beloved dog whereas now it seems that Willow has been given a new lease of life!

If you'd like to know more about how these therapies could be used to support an animal in your life please get in touch:

robyn@equenergy.com — 07980 669303

For Reiki and META-Health information you can see my website:

www.equenergy.com

For information on Botanical Self-Healing, see:

www.myanimalmatters.co.uk

N.B. do not offer fats to a dog with a history of pancreatitis.
Remedies should be offered for self-selection only and not added to their food or water.

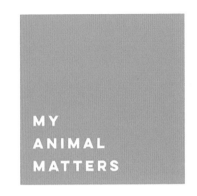

MY
ANIMAL
MATTERS

TESTED BY ANIMALS

AAFCO STANDARDS

A Worthless Measure
for determining the Nutritional Value of Pet Foods?

by Ian Billinghurst

Foods for companion animals — How do we assess their value? Are the rules any different for real food vs the fake industrial products produced by the processed pet food industry? What sort of reliance should we place on the AAFCO standards?

INTRODUCTION

There are many different food types produced for companion animals. In this article I will talk about just two — found at opposite ends of the health spectrum. In doing so and for the sake of convenience, I will refer to foods for companion animals — our domestic cats and dogs — as "pet foods".

The first pet food type is produced by the major multinational pet food companies —under the auspices of AAFCO. These are highly denatured products — produced largely from industrial waste — they are principally dry foods. However, whether wet or dry, they are all dependent on carbohydrates as their principal energy source. The carbohydrates are generally derived from grain, and often contain gluten. These non-genomic, non-evolutionary foods are best described as Fake Industrial Foods (FIF's).

The second food type may be produced at home or by small niche companies. These foods are formulated according to evolutionary principles. These foods are derived, principally from (raw) animal sources, together with fresh vegetable material, and reflect the range and balance of the raw and whole foods domestic cats and dogs evolved to require. They are minimally processed and rely on fats and proteins as their principal energy source. They are never grain-based and are generally referred to as RAW (foods).

In relation to these two vastly different food types, there is a question for which nobody appears to have an authoritative answer. "Do the AAFCO standards — as detailed in the writings published by AAFCO — apply to properly formulated, raw, whole foods? This is a vitally important question because the failure to comply with AAFCO standards is a common accusation leveled at raw foods; it deters many would be raw feeders from making the switch; thus compromising their dog's health.

As we seek answers to this question, we discover that AAFCO is not what so many people believe it to be — and this takes us way beyond the original question. Most particularly we discover that raw foods easily pass the AAFCO tests — and in doing so — demonstrate the irrelevance of the AAFCO standards in relation to not only RAW, but also the fake industrial foods for pets.

VETS NUTRITION AND AAFCO

Veterinarians seek reliance and certainty in all that they say, do and recommend, and look to science as the final authority in these matters. However, as professionals, they must be careful in the choice of the science they choose to believe and/or accept as their authority.

In the case of small animal nutrition, veterinarians have a problem. The guidebook, the rule book, the AAFCO set of rules that vets rely on for their companion animal nutritional information, is a long way from being based on the sound science that vets would like — and *assume* — it to be.

The almost universal veterinary assumption is that the AAFCO standards provide absolute certainty and authority when it comes to companion animal nutrition.

Today, the vast majority of Vets, vet nurses, pet food producers, breeders, concerned owners — in fact, most anyone with a professional or personal interest or concern with the welfare, health and nutrition of companion cats and dogs —looks to AAFCO — the Association of American Feed Control Officials — to provide the standards, the guiding nutritional light, the basic principles on which food for companion animals should be formulated.

The current and universal belief amongst members of the veterinary profession is that if a product states on its label that its contents conform to AAFCO standards, this is all we need to know in order to have absolute faith in the nutritional integrity of that product. The assumption is — that product will provide all the nutrients the cat or dog requires and in a form and balance that will ensure optimal assimilation. As a result, this product is assumed to ensure perfect health for the life-stage and activity level of its intended consumer. These assumptions include the belief that this product will produce in its consumer, the greatest possible longevity and freedom from degenerative disease processes.

There is an urgent need to question this faith, this authority

And the first fact I will point to is that around ninety to ninety five percent of dogs or cats suffering from cancer, autoimmune disease, allergies, renal failure, inflammatory bowel disease, lower urinary tract disease, in fact any degenerative disease process you care to name, has developed this problem following a lifetime consumption of industrial foods — foods that have fulfilled all the requirements to make them AAFCO compliant.

FAKE INDUSTRIAL FOOD — BASED ON FLAWED SCIENCE

No matter how it is dressed up, no matter how fine the language that is used, the science that underpins the AAFCO standards — and the production of food that follows those standards — is flawed science. A close examination of the AAFCO book of standards — as it applies to dogs and cats — reveals a disturbing picture ranging from complete not knowing all the way through to uncertainty, guesses, qualifications, explanatory footnotes — and a propensity to continually shift the goal posts.

The AAFCO guide makes no mention of whole raw foods. This is no accident. Its authors make no bones about the fact that this is a book whose sole purpose is to detail the use of sub-standard materials in the construction of industrial pet food (they don't use those exact words but that is what they mean). This guide is designed only for the pet food manufacturer who is reliant on such inferior materials; which includes — sadly — the vast majority of pet food manufacturers in the world today.

The AAFCO guide is of no value to anyone wishing to know how to feed genuinely healthy foods to their dogs or cats. The standards it details apply only to products that are best described as industrial waste. These standards fall well short of the high standards that evolutionary nutrition imposes on its adherents.

RAW MOVES BEYOND AAFCO

In contrast to the science, which explains how to make poor quality material into sub-standard foods for our furry family members, the science that underpins or supports evolutionary nutrition explains how to develop programmes of nutrition from whole raw healthy nutritious foods. Such foods not only fulfill AAFCO standards — and easily pass its feeding protocols —They move way beyond those standards.

AAFCO — AKIN TO RELIGIOUS FAITH

When it comes to formulating pet food, what we find today is that most people who are involved with cats and dogs — including most particularly the vast majority of the veterinary profession —have what might best be described as a type of unquestioning — almost spiritual — or perhaps religious might be a better word — faith in the AAFCO nutritional standards. That faith and that unquestioning set of assumptions, ignores the stated purpose of the AAFCO guidelines. It is assumed that these guidelines relate — ALSO — to actual whole and fresh foods. They do not.

The AAFCO rulebook has been elevated to the status of holy writ in relation to companion animal nutrition.

Apart from the bible itself, the only other book held in such awe and reverence that I can remember — is the "Junior Woodchucks Guidebook". This was the book that Disney's cartoon characters — Huey, Dewey and Louie — looked to whenever they needed rock-solid and detailed information on any subject you could possibly imagine: kinda — the 1950's version of google.

These days, when I speak to vet students about nutrition, their faith in AAFCO — and its guidebook — gives me this feeling that I am speaking to Huey, Dewey and Louie. The only difference being, not one of these students has ever actually consulted this complex, contradictory and misleading guide.

MANNA FROM HEAVEN?

This widespread conviction, this unwavering belief in the infallibility of AAFCO and its rules is of enormous concern. Much of that concern relates to the deep sense of trust that today's aspiring vets — Huey, Dewey and Louie — place in the integrity of the fake industrial foods developed in response to the AAFCO standards.

Are these foods really manna from heaven? Should we really place this level of faith in the Junior Wood-chuck's Guide?

As you will see, this is a faith and a trust that has no foundation in fact and to begin the discussion, we need to expand our discussion on the AAFCO standards and ask three important questions.

THREE IMPORTANT QUESTIONS

Do AAFCO standards apply to RAW pet foods?

The First and most important question we need to discuss and answer, is whether the AAFCO standards — as written in the AAFCO rule-book — have any value or legitimacy in relation to raw whole foods. The answer to this question will surprise many of the most ardent of raw feeders.

Do AAFCO standards apply to ANY pet food?

The second question is whether the AAFCO written standards are of any value in determining the nutritional status of the industrial food they are designed to help formulate. Unfortunately, even here, they are of little value. How can a food that starts out using sub-standard materials be valuable nutritionally?

What value are the AAFCO feeding trials?

This third question asks whether the AAFCO feeding trials are any sort of accurate or reliable measure of the nutritional value of ANY pet food — whether it is a fake industrial product or a raw food? The answer to this question is not as most people (including most members of the veterinary profession) fondly believe.

To find legitimate answers these three questions, we will begin with some AAFCO basics.

AAFCO BASICS

AAFCO LABELING REQUIREMENTS

To get some sort of understanding of how AAFCO

operates, we need to get hold of a bag of fake industrial dog food and examine the AAFCO labeling claims and the AAFCO statements found on those bags or packs. It is these CLAIMS, THESE STATEMENTS, THESE WORDS, that Huey, Dewey and Louie PLACE SUCH RELIANCE UPON — AND LOOK TO — as their assurance of nutritional perfection.

Ask any young vet today and you will be told that the AAFCO prescribed labeling of a dog food is designed to confirm, to assure and give comfort to the pet owning public. Label statements are designed to (and must) tell us the basic and vital information we need to know about the bag's contents.

CLAIM ONE — COMPLETE AND BALANCED?

The first claim that must be made by the manufacturer relates to the issue of completeness and balance. We must look for the label claim that says the product has been formulated to be complete and balanced according to AAFCO. Once we read those words, we can happily feed the product, fully confident that it contains every nutrient our dog requires.

Well, that's what our young vets are taught to think — or perhaps believe would be a better word — because when it comes to nutrition — vets believe they no longer have to think. All they need is unwavering faith. Yes, pet food has been raised to the status of religious faith — no questioning or doubts allowed!

Let's look more closely at this — give these words and claims a little thought.

The word "complete"

What the word "complete" is actually telling us is that this pet food contains every nutrient that AAFCO currently deems as essential for its intended consumer.

Unfortunately, this has nothing to do with what that consumer actually requires — in a biological sense. All it tells us is that the product conforms to a standard of completeness as designed and currently approved by an AAFCO committee. This standard is different to the myriad AAFCO standards that have been promulgated as scientific fact over the past decades. And, given this climate of continually shifting goal posts — there is an iron-clad certainty — this standard will not apply next week or next year and certainly not by next decade.

The word "balanced"

The word "balanced" means that those (aforementioned) nutrients are present in the proportions as currently approved by AAFCO — and — once again — this is a claim that lacks biological validity,

AND — once again — there is every chance that the goal posts will be moved in the not too distant future.

Clearly, our dog's and our cat's evolutionary (or genomic)
nutritional requirements have not changed over these decades,
just AAFCO's current (and continually flawed) understanding.

I need to make this point most strongly because every year — the rulebook is up-dated. Last years rules do not necessarily apply this year. This freedom or necessity to change the goal posts does not apply to feeding raw, where the nutritional rules are sound and remain valid and constant from year to year.

It gets worse. When you actually read AAFCO in detail, you realize — in fact they tell you — that the levels they prescribe – for many nutrients — are at best a compromise — and at worst a guess — being based on nothing more than opinion.

This is very poor science. In fact, it is NOT science.

Even more problematic is the fact that we (the scientific community in general and AAFCO in particular) do not as yet have a full list of the nutrients that our companion animals require, or their ideal proportions. This makes the claim of completeness and balance totally invalid from a biological point of view. The best we can say of fake industrial foods for dogs is that they are legally complete and balanced. This is in total contrast to the raw feeding paradigm, where properly formulated raw whole food is in fact both legally and biologically complete and balanced.

The health implications of this are enormous.

CLAIM TWO — LIFE STAGE?

The second claim AAFCO wants the label to make relates to the suitability of the product in relation to canine life stage. Is this product suitable to feed a growing pup for example, or is it only suitable to maintain a dog once it has finished growing, in which case it is called a MAINTENANCE food.

Maintenance

Think about this. Maintenance refers to a formulation

that — according to AAFCO — will NOT adequately support, growth, reproduction or lactation.

This INABILITY signals — that maintenance food is the poorest of the poor — and begs the question — "Why would you even consider feeding this sort of sub-standard food to your dog or cat?

Real food – suitable for all life stages

Compare this to feeding raw whole foods — evolutionary nutrition. Real foods, when properly formulated — according to the very simple and basic principles of evolutionary nutrition — are suitable for every life stage, every breed and every type of activity.

Better yet, we can also formulate prescription diets from raw. And these programmes will deal — far more satisfactorily — with any disease state — compared to the industrial prescription stuff. These programmes not only deal with the physiological malfunction involved, but unlike the industrial stuff, which at best can only slow the degenerative process, raw foods also begin to repair the damage caused by that process. These are genuinely healing foods.

In other words — prescription diets are better than brilliant — when constructed from raw.

Claim three – method used to substantiate

The third issue that AAFCO want you to know about — AND which therefore must be on the label — is to confirm the method that was used to substantiate the first two claims. On this point it is important to appreciate that AAFCO only accepts two methods of testing foods in order for them to proudly boast they are AAFCO approved or AAFCO compliant… the *analytical* method and the *feeding trial* method.

The analytical method

The first method is by analysis — where the food is chemically analyzed to substantiate its adherence to AAFCO's standards.

This is a highly questionable process. Its results provide very little of value in ascertaining the nutritional value of any food sample. For example, a food made from a mixture of cardboard (carbohydrate), together with any type of leather (protein), sump oil (fat), blood and bone fertilizer (protein and minerals including calcium) — to which is added a premix of vitamins and minerals — would pass this test with flying colours.

The feeding trial

The second way to test the food for AAFCO compliance is by an AAFCO approved feeding trial; these are trials that must be conducted according to specific AAFCO protocols. And — IF — that sounds like a concern — in terms of complexity and difficulty — there is no cause for alarm. The trials are simplicity in the extreme.

On the other hand, if that sounds like a concern — in terms of a lack of scientific validity — of leniency and ease of passage and the possibility that the trial will mostly fail to pick up on a poor quality dog food — the concern is legitimate.

The AAFCO trials are deeply flawed; they lack scientific validity.

This means that no matter which way the products are tested, the fact that a product is AAFCO approved is no guarantee of its nutritional integrity, or its ability to maintain the health of its intended consumer. But perhaps those of us who are raw feeders already knew that!

This brings us to the point where we need to explain and enlarge on the fundamental difference between these two pet food paradigms — fake industrial food vs Raw food. And I will begin this discussion by noting that — (unfortunately) — most producers of RAW pet foods today are constrained by legalities to make these AAFCO claims. And yet the only claim they should be making is that their product conforms to the principles of evolutionary nutrition and on that basis is not only legally complete and balanced but is — more importantly — complete and balanced in a biological sense.

TWO CONTRASTING PARADIGMS

What we are dealing with here — when we compare RAW with fake industrial pet food — are two totally different and incompatible paradigms, based on totally contrasting forms of scientific evidence.

This is a contrast between flawed science, structured to reach or produce a desired outcome, and real science, based on a genuine curiosity, that asks — "What is the truth and why is it so?"

We will FIRST look at the **Industrial Food Programme** — and the questionable "Science" that supports it.

FAKE INDUSTRIAL FOOD

The products, which together constitute this group of pet foods, were introduced without any form of scientific verification or any desire to produce healthy dogs.

These products are based on just one desire — the necessity to turn industrial waste into $$$$'s

The industrial programme was introduced with no scientific scrutiny, research or verification; various industry groups with no training in canine (or feline) nutrition introduced the idea. These people decided that the wastes of the human food industry, together with stock food and by products normally used to produce fertilizer, could be converted into valuable dollars by creating dog (and cat) food.

And so the pet food industry was born.

Since that time, the only science applied to these products has been flawed or non-science science. This so-called science — the scientific basis of AAFCO — may be outlined or described as follows…

THE FLAWED SCIENCE
Underpinning AAFCO's "Rules"

Committee of "experts"

The first bit of science involved is to elect a committee of nutritional experts.

These nutritional experts must reach consensus on a set of standards. These standards must be based on National Research Council guidelines; and they must involve the so-called "commonly" used ingredients, because as AFFCO writers admit, anything less nutritionally compromised, would be way too expensive to include in a commercially produced pet food.

Commonly used ingredients

These commonly used ingredients include a prescribed list of protein sources, carbohydrate sources, fat sources and fiber sources — all of which have been or will be heat treated — and which are basically waste products of other industries. These are the materials from which fake industrial foods for cats and dogs will be constructed — chosen chiefly for their cheapness and availability.

Virtually none of these food sources could — in any way — be regarded as fresh and wholesome (if we were feeding humans for example).

The only additive required will be some form of vitamin and mineral premix that conforms to a standard (as decided by that same group of so-called nutritional experts). This premix MUST be added because the waste material being used, apart from containing seriously compromised fat and protein sources and being full of unnecessary carbohydrates (nutritionally speaking) is seriously lacking in most essential vitamins and minerals, not to mention the protective nutrients found in fresh whole foods.

THE PRESUMPTIONS UNDERPINNING THE PRODUCTION OF FAKE INDUSTRIAL FOOD

Every bit of scientific research that underpins the production of fake industrial food for dogs and cats is built on a basic set of presumptions or premises — these are premises that are commonly accepted as valid.

We will now examine these presumptions — and ask the question: … "Can we accept them as valid?"

1) Rawness or heat-treated is irrelevant

The **first** presumption — underpinning the production of fake industrial food under the guidance of the AAFCO rulebook — is that Rawness or cooked-ness is irrelevant in the production of healthy pet foods.

AAFCO admits that the materials used to produce these foods are all highly heat-treated and therefore compromised nutritionally — but they presuppose this will be accounted for — by adding supplements.

2) This food contains every essential nutrient

And so the **second** presumption — is that this group of materials — together with the prescribed supplements — that in no way represents what the ancestors of our domestic dogs and cats have eaten — and that is highly compromised nutritionally — **contains everything** our dogs and cats needs in terms of nutrition. This is not science — in actuality it is an enormous leap of faith, particularly given presumption no three.

3) Any substance not on the list - has no nutritional value

This **third** presumption — which is that any substance **not listed** in the AAFCO standards has **absolutely no nutritional value** for a dog or a cat — demonstrates the scientific ignorance and arrogance of the AAFCO approach to nutrition. This non-scientific approach to nutrition is further compromised by the fourth presumption…

4) Mixing and heating these materials does not compromise nutrition

The **fourth** presumption — is that **mixing** the prescribed materials together **and** then **cooking** them has **no bearing on** the **nutritional value** of the final product — even though it is well established that the chemical interactions that occur at the high temperatures used to make pet food not only render many nutrients unavailable, but also produce toxins, mutagens and carcinogens. If that were not bad enough for the health of our companion animals, it is made worse by presumption number five.

5) Carbs as principle energy source? … *No worries!*

The **fifth** presumption is that the principal energy source — **carbohydrates** — used in fake industrial foods for pets — has no bearing on their health. This ignores the fact that the ancestors of our dogs and cats derived their energy principally from fats and proteins. Their whole metabolism is geared to respond to energy produced principally from these two sources. The Hills Company makes this very point in literature upholding the merits of its "metabolic" diet for dogs.

6) All committee decisions are *final & valid* …

The **sixth** presumption is that the **decisions** made by the AAFCO committee of nutritional experts, are final and **valid** and truly represent a dog's or a cat's nutritional needs at every stage of its life and for every activity it might be called upon to perform.

This appearance of stability and of eternal scientific truth — written in stone — as assumed by most members of the veterinary profession — together with most lay people involved with dogs and/or cats — is highly deceptive. There is no stability. This is not the final word. This is definitely not scientific truth. It is in fact not science at all, it is simply a compromise based on the various opinions of the committee members — as they currently stand. AAFCO'S inability to provide meaningful or valid information is further compromised by the seventh presumption — which states …

7) All rules are subject to change

So here we have written in a guidebook — produced by AAFCO — supposedly eternal scientific truths — that are in actuality, ideas that are ephemeral and transient making them not only unreliable and invalid, but in many ways useless and potentially dangerous. They most certainly do not represent nutritional truth.

8) Analysis of pet foods — a foolproof safeguard?

This brings us to the **eighth** presumption — underpinning the AAFCO rule book — which is that a food must be tested to ensure that all currently accepted as essential nutrients are present in that product and that they are present at the AAFCO designated levels.

One way to test this is by analysis; unfortunately testing a food by analysis is riddled with potential errors.

Analysis totally disregards any bioavailability issues. It ignores the fact that what is being tested for is subject to constant change, and it is made totally redundant by AAFCO principle number nine, that says we must — under certain prescribed conditions — totally ignore the fact that a food has failed the analytical test.

Let's look at that one more closely…

9) A successful feeding trial negates an analytical fail

Presumption number **nine** states that — "No matter how badly the analysis of any particular food fails AAFCO written standards, this fact may be totally ignored if the food in question has successfully passed the AAFCO feeding trials". In other words, all of the AAFCO rules may be thrown out the window if a product — despite having failed AAFCO's analytical test — can pass the AAFCO prescribed feeding trials.

This AAFCO principle tells us that the hundreds of pages of complex nutritional rules and regulations that AAFCO uses to explain how to make pet food from industrial waste, is actually of little practical value — and is in fact — literally meaningless.

And I suspect that many raw feeders would not be surprised — and saying amen — to that!

And let me go a little bit further and say that this ninth principle is in fact the only presumption that has some semblance of scientific merit. I say semblance because as you will see, although any properly formulated raw whole food diet will easily pass an AAFCO feeding trial, so do a whole range of nutritionally inadequate fake industrial foods — and by that I mean — products that come into the category of the worst of the worst.

10) Improving dog foods by feeding trials

And speaking of feeding trials, this brings us to the **tenth** presumption underpinning the industrial pet food paradigm. This presumption involves the production of better pet food through research programmes.

The pet food industry carries out so-called "scientific research", where it uses feeding trials to pit one fake industrial food against another. These trials are designed to tell us, which of these (poor quality) products is better than the other.

The net result is that we find out which is the supposed) best of a bad lot! This is a classic example of the non-science, used by the pet food companies to persuade us that we are feeding our dogs and cats the best food possible and this fact has been verified by the soundest of scientific research. This approach continues to fool most people — including an entire veterinary profession… which falls for this non-science — hook-line and sinker!

This incredibly bad science brings us to principle number elven.

11) No research to genuinely look at RAW

The **eleventh** principle is the same as the tenth only stated differently. It says that a manufacturer will never conduct a feeding trial — that pits a raw food against an industrial food. This sounds like I am being facetious, but the truth is, such trials never happen.

No manufacturer of fake industrial food has ever carried out trials to compare its fake industrial product with any form of properly formulated raw whole food.

If a manufacturer of industrial food did this, it would be valid science. However, such research is never conducted. Such research would tell a manufacturer of fake industrial food something he or she knows but does not want to have verified scientifically…

"That raw whole foods are in fact exactly what he or she should be manufacturing, recommending and selling!"

This brings us to the final principle that underpins the industrial food paradigm. Rather than conduct studies to determine if the raw paradigm has merit, research is carried out with the stated aim of discrediting raw.

12) Research designed to discredit raw

The **twelth** presumption underpinning the whole fake industrial food paradigm, is that it is good science to conduct research with the stated aim of discrediting raw. One example is the research conducted to demonstrate the presence of bacteria in raw food. The conclusion from this is that because these bacteria belong to a group or family of bacteria, some members of which, have the potential to be harmful, raw foods will cause severe and even fatal illness to our dogs or cats as well as to the people handling the food, or to people coming into contact with the animal in question or its feces, its saliva and so on.

Unfortunately, this has not been followed up with further research — conducted to determine whether properly constructed and handled raw pet food — and there is plenty of it out there now — has actually, in practice, caused the problems that it has been conjectured to (supposedly) cause — given the likely presence of potential pathogens.
Those of us who have recommended raw food as vets, and used raw food as pet owners or carers, know that these accusations are without foundation. However, they have an enormous influence on many people, deterring them from feeding raw.

Within the flawed science that supports the production of fake industrial food — as overseen by the AAFCO rule book and outlined above — there is one aspect I want to discuss in a little more detail — the quality of the materials used to make fake industrial food.

THE QUALITY OF MATERIALS USED TO CONSTRUCT FAKE INDUSTRIAL FOODS… the AAFCO — commonly used ingredients…

AAFCO has made it clear in numerous publications that their aim is to establish practical nutrient profiles for both dog and cat foods "based on commonly used ingredients."

Note the words "based on commonly used ingredients."

If we check on what AAFCO considers "commonly used ingredients" in fake industrial foods for pets, we find from their publications that they mean items such as…

- Meat and bone meal
- Chicken by-product meal
- Fishmeal
- Chicken liver meal
- Peanut hulls
- Cellulose
- Soybean hulls
- Vegetable oil … and so on

Understanding the terms on pet food labels

All of these commonly used ingredients are compromised nutritionally — and AAFCO admits this in their writings. They accept that this is the material that pet food manufacturers work with and base their recommendations on such materials.

Food labeling is meant to inform the purchaser about the product; however, the manufacturer sees the label as an opportunity to obfuscate and deceive (the non pejorative term for this is "marketing").

For example, most people, having read the word "chicken" on a pet food label, immediately picture a fresh whole chicken and they naturally assume the product contains a balanced combination of fresh chicken flesh, skin and possibly bone. The packaging often has a picture of piece of fresh raw chicken to consolidate this thinking. Sadly, this is a long way from the truth. To understand what is actually meant — note the use of the words "by-product" and "meal" — commonly found in association with the word chicken.

"By-product"

If we find the words "by-product" in the descriptor, this means that the so-called "chicken" will be mostly bones or heads or feet – heat treated of course – making the product not only of low nutritional value but highly indigestible as well. It may also mean just **feathers**! Yes truly!

"Meal"

The inclusion of the word "meal" in the descriptor means that following cooking and drying, this material is finely ground. One reason for grinding is to disguise the fact that this product is composed chiefly of cooked bone, which is VERY cheap to buy (feathers are even cheaper).

While raw meaty bones are brilliant food for dogs and cats, this is not the case once they have been cooked and rendered. This is a process that subjects these bones to extreme temperatures over long periods of time. The net result is a product with very little nutritional value. What protein remains is practically indigestible and the calcium is in a form that is highly inappropriate and causes bone problems in growing animals, most particularly the giant breeds of dogs..

No relationship with raw whole foods

Basically, these materials bear no relationship to the RAW, WHOLE and ACTUAL food materials our companion animals evolved eating. For example, all the protein-source items on that list (such as meat and bone meal, chicken by-product meal, fish meal or chicken liver meal) have been subjected to extremely high temperatures prior to their use in pet food. And they will be cooked yet again to produce the finished product.

Highly denatured

This repeated heat assault means that pet parents buying industrial foods are feeding their dogs or cats a product with highly denatured proteins and heat-damaged fats. Worse yet, many of the components — have reacted chemically with each other producing substances that are not only indigestible and therefore useless, but are in numerous cases toxic, mutagenic and carcinogenic. These chemical reactions further damage these nutritionally depleted products with the loss of both vitamins and minerals.

Bioavailability issues

The AAFCO writers note in a recent publication, that all the raw materials — and the word "raw" is actually a misnomer — used to produce industrial pet foods have bioavailability issues, relating to both the origin of these materials and their denaturation by heat.

Nutrient levels — no reliable guidelines

On this basis the AAFCO writers further note that because of these problems, it is actually very difficult to establish nutrient levels that can be relied upon. What they are actually saying is that when you work with biologically inappropriate materials, it is almost impossible to produce valid and reliable guidelines.

As an example of this problem, I will now quote from a recent AAFCO publication —which reads as follows …

"The specific example for iron can be generalized to most essential minerals and demonstrates the impossibility — that any list of concentrations can invariably ensure — that all nutrient requirements are fulfilled — in all diet formulas … ".

Basically they are saying — we simply don't know, but we will have a guess.

AAFCO cites numerous factors affecting mineral digestibility including: specific source of the mineral, the concentration of other minerals in the mix, the presence of other ingredients, as well as the mineral status of the animal eating the food.

And then there is the issue of calcium.

This inability to give valid guidelines includes the issue of calcium. The calcium derived from cooked bones — as found in fake industrial foods is not assimilated in the same way as the calcium in raw bone. In growing animals this can — and often does — form part of the problems that produces the bone and joint diseases we see in our dogs, most especially the larger breeds that routinely dine on these fake products.

These problems include hip and elbow dysplasia, together with a whole host of related bone and joint problems — including arthritis — so common in older dogs fed these industrial products.

Think on this. The AAFCO publications are telling us that for essential nutrients, such as calcium iron, magnesium, zinc, manganese, selenium and so on — they — AAFCO — have insufficient data to establish maximum or minimum levels or an optimal level for any of these minerals. The bottom line here is that the AAFCO is in no position to judge — using its rulebook — the validity or otherwise of a raw food product. However, it gets worse. As we shall see, the feeding trials as advocated by AAFCO, make total nonsense of the rulebook in terms of not only raw foods, but also the fake industrial foods themselves.

In short, AAFCO's recommendations or standards for mineral levels in pet foods are a nutritional compromise; an arbitrary figure employing numerous assumptions including a random value for digestibility. Basically, they are having a GUESS. It gets worse. The AAFCO writers, not only admit their inability to give valid and meaningful levels of minerals in their guidelines, they make similar admissions for vitamin levels.

Knowing this — how can we possibly place any faith in the AAFCO rules in the way that — currently — our veterinary profession is doing.

And remember, these AAFCO recommendations (as useless as they are) are for foods where all the ingredients are highly compromised in terms of freshness, wholeness and rawness. Most importantly – and this is the take-home point – these "guesses" are NOT necessary when we feed properly constructed RAW.

Because AAFCO is unable to give valid and meaningful levels of minerals in its guidelines, this clearly disqualifies the AAFCO guidelines as having any validity in relation to the foods it oversees, let alone raw whole foods.

Real whole raw foods work with our cat and dog's homeostatic mechanisms to produce the perfect results we are seeking in terms of completeness, balance and biologically appropriate availability.

*This is **sound science** — based on a genuine understanding of the nutrition that our pet's bodies cry out for.*

Veterinary profession – absolute trust in this invalid material

And having made this point let me take you back to a point I made earlier. It is these invalid and unreliable guidelines, this invalid set of rules that our veterinary profession is prepared to quote, to believe in to place on the pedestal of holy writ, and use as their authority when advising pet owners on how and with what they should feed their dogs.

AAFCO and their set of rules is also what many vets will use to tell us that the raw food products we use to feed our dogs are failing to comply with accepted standards.

This approach to nutrition by the veterinary profession needs to change.

AAFCO ADMITS

Its Written Standards Do Not Apply to Raw Foods

AAFFCO freely admits its written standards apply only to Fake Industrial Foods

By specifying that its rule book applies specifically to "commonly used ingredients", and by specifically ruling out the use of more expensive and more bio-available ingredients — AAFCO is acknowledging – perhaps unwittingly – that their standards in no way relate to the materials used to construct RAW WHOLE foods.

In other words — and this is important, when it comes to AAFCO's highly complicated rule book, which specifies amounts and levels of nutrients in the most detailed of terms — AAFCO is saying that its standards relate or apply ONLY to fake industrial foods.

Feeding trials – a different matter

However, while it is clear that the written standards only apply to fake industrial foods, the feeding protocols are a different matter entirely — and we are going to enlarge on this vital and surprising topic shortly!

DETERMINING NUTRITIONAL ADEQUACY

I now want to return to the heart of the matter… the fact that AAFCO recognizes just two ways to substantiate the nutritional adequacy of a pet food.

AAFCO's Analytical Fiasco

As we know — the first way AAFCO substantiates a food's ability to support life, health, reproductive ability and longevity is by analysis. This analytical method ensures that the nutrient profile is consistent with AAFCO standards. Note that AAFCO only includes those nutrients — in its standards — that it recognizes as essential.

Apart from the obvious fact that analysis tells us nothing about the actual availability of these nutrients for the consumer, it should also be noted that the list is limited to currently accepted (by AAFCO) "essential" nutrients. For example, it places no value on the presence of phytonutrients — and I cannot help but emphasise that particular flaw — because of the well known science telling us it is these nutrients, which have such a powerful role to play in reducing the ravages of degenerative disease, most especially cancer — and we are all aware as people who care passionately about our cat and dog family members, of the levels of cancer they now suffer — which are now essentially the same as ours!

The second way for these products to gain AAFCO approval is for the product to pass the AAFCO feeding protocols. And as we have seen, AAFCO makes it clear … where a product is substantiated as nutritionally adequate by feeding trials… that product does not have to meet the AAFCO nutrient profile standards — making a complete nonsense of those standards!

That latter FACT is actually supportive and highly relevant
to anyone wishing to feed raw…

Feeding trials will validate genuine raw

As those of us who feed raw know only too well, any properly formulated RAW product, when subjected to long-term feeding trials, will be found, at the very least, to be nutritionally adequate. And THIS WILL BE SO FOR ALL LIFE STAGES. And most importantly, AAFCO itself recognizes that where this is so, their nutrient profiles are irrelevant. In other words, AAFCO accepts that under these circumstances, their standards can be abandoned.

From the point of view of the RAW feeder, the very obvious reason for this (not obvious to AAFCO) is the limited scope and limited availability of the nutrients found in fake industrial food, in no way compares to the broad range and biologically correct availability of nutrients derived from RAW WHOLE FOODS.

This brings me back to emphasizing the point that the standards imposed on fake industrial foods by AAFCO bear very little relevance to the standards that raw whole foods must adhere to.

AAFCO's complicated rules vs feeding trials

If we give any thought to all of this, we have to conclude that the AAFCO feeding trials make their written standards irrelevant and meaningless. To allow a feeding trial to out-vote an analysis based on AAFCO's written standards is a most powerful admission by AAFCO that they have no real idea of what the feeding standards for cats and dogs should be.

This has enormous implications for the reliance we place on those standards when you consider something I mentioned earlier — that the vast majority, in fact close to one hundred percent of pets suffering from cancer, autoimmune disease, allergies, renal failure, inflammatory bowel disease, in fact any degenerative disease process you care to name, has developed this problem following a lifetime consumption of food that has passed the AAFCO standards.

Clearly, there are a lot of reasons for this and we have discussed some of the most important ones. And one of the most important contributors is and will continue to be the feeding trials developed by AAFCO

Feeding trials – hard to fail!

The feeding trials as prescribed by AAFCO are designed in such a way that they allow even the most nutritionally marginal Fake Industrial Food to pass with flying colours. In other words, a product has to be monumentally woeful in order to fail the AAFCO feeding trials.

Even a cursory examination of the AAFCO feeding trials illustrates this point with alarming clarity…

AAFCO FEEDING TRIALS OR PROTOCOLS

As previously pointed out AAFCO feeding trial may be used in place of a nutritional analysis to verify a food as conforming to the AAFCO nutritional standards.

These trials may be summarized as follows …

1. The feeding trial is valid if it contains at least 8 animals. *(Note that such a small number of participants is not considered as able to produce statistically significant results, particularly given parameters 2, 3 & 4.)*

2. Breed and/or sex is irrelevant

3. Two animals in the trial may drop out — for whatever reason

4. The trial need only last for 26 weeks.

5. The only food available to the animals participating in the trial is the food being tested.

6. Good quality water must be available at all times.

7. Prior to the trial, and at the end of the trial, each animal must be examined physically by a veterinarian and be pronounced healthy in terms of its general health, its bodily condition and the condition of its hair and coat.

8. When the trial is over, there are four blood values that must be measured (these are NOT measured before the trial begins). These blood parameters are …

    a) Haemoglobin levels

    b) Packed cell volume (PCV)

    c) The enzyme "Serum alkaline phosphatase

    d) Serum albumin

For each of these blood values there are specified minimums. In assessing the animals in the trial, the values recorded by the animals are averaged. So long as the average value is greater than the specified minimums, the food passes the test.

If you give all of this any thought, it is clear that the feeding trial is designed in such a way that almost ANY food would pass!

So the next question is — what would cause a food to fail the test?

HOW CAN A FOOD FAIL THE AAFCO FEEDING TRIALS?

Parameters for failure

For the diet being tested to fail requires that it demonstrate one or more of the following problems…

    1. Some form of Nutritional deficiency or excess

        In this case, one (or more) of the animals being tested must show clinical signs of a nutritional deficiency or excess.

2. Loss of more than 15% Bodyweight

Here — that one or more of the animals being tested must lose more than 15% of its starting bodyweight

3. Any blood value being less than the specified minimum

And finally — one or more of the blood value averages falls below the specified minimum level.

Clearly this is a very minimal set of standards. The bar has been set way too low!

The AAFCO trial is a very poor trial indeed

All any food has to do — is keep 6 out of 8 apparently healthy dogs alive for 26 weeks without …

- Any of them losing more than 15% of their bodyweight and

- Without there being any signs of nutritional deficiency or excess and …

- Without the average of four basic blood parameters falling below a specified level

Minimal testing…

There is no examination of urine or stools, no examination of white cells, urea, Creatinine, glucose, total protein, sodium, potassium, bicarbonate or other tests routinely performed by veterinarians as a health screening test.

Nutritional deficiency – difficult to achieve!

It is most important to note that it would be a very poor dog food that would result in massive weight loss, or the failure to meet any one of those four blood parameters or for a nutritional deficiency to surface in an adult dog in a period of six months.

Fake industrial foods – an easy passage

Clearly, these trials set a very low standard. A product would have to be pretty bad to fail an AAFCO feeding trial.

Let me repeat — the AAFCO feeding trials have been designed…
to allow poor quality foods to pass.

And yet it is theses tests that vets accept as the "Gold

Standard" way to test a pet food for its safety and reliability and health enhancing abilities.

On this basis, it is also reasonable to conclude that any properly formulated raw food would easily pass such a poorly designed trial.

Which brings us back to RAW foods —aka Evolutionary Nutrition …

THE EVOLUTIONARY NUTRITIONAL PARADIGM

Let us now examine the scientific basis — AND THE SIMPLICITY —of the Evolutionary programme of nutrition

What Is Evolutionary Nutrition?

Feeding the diet an animal evolved to require

Very briefly, the Evolutionary program of nutrition is about feeding animals the diet they evolved to require. This programme is based on the principles of Darwinian evolution, the same principles that underpin molecular biology, the sequencing of the genome and modern medical science. This is real science — not fake industrial food science.

How is evolutionary nutrition formulated?

The formulation of any Evolutionary Programme of Nutrition depends on knowing the range and balance of those whole raw foods an animal evolved to eat over the millions of years of its genetic adaptation. This is a programme that has genomic fit. This is genuinely valid nutritional science.

THE BASIC PRINCIPLES OF EVOLUTIONARY NUTRITION

The Principles underpinning the evolutionary paradigm are …

The Food Must be Raw and Unprocessed

The **first** principle underpinning the Evolutionary or RAW program of nutrition is that the components are for the most part presented in their raw unprocessed form, making them — completely bioavailable — to the extent —and in the form — that the animal or species in question requires.

To put that another way, the bioavailability of the component parts has genomic fit. This is in complete contrast to the materials used to construct fake industrial food, not one of which is fed raw or unprocessed.

Duplication or - as close as possible to Evolutionary Food

The **second** principle — is that the materials used — either duplicate — or mimic as closely as possible — the whole raw foods that the ancestors of the animal in question would have eaten. Again, this is the polar opposite to the situation that occurs with fake industrial foods, where the components in no way represent the foods that dogs have eaten over the last few million years.

No list of required nutrients

The **third** principle is that there is no list of required nutrients. These are not required — firstly because we simply don't need to know this information and secondly, because this information is not actually known. What the evolutionary programme depends upon is the obvious fact that the food an animal's ancestors evolves eating — contains by definition — every nutrient it requires — both known and unknown. What we also know is that homeostatic mechanisms — when combined with foods with genomic fit — ensure proper nutritional balance. Nothing could be simpler.

And this leads us straight into the next principle ...

No requirement for detailed rules

The **fourth** principle is that there is no requirement for the detailed rules of nutrition as imposed by AAFCO. And clearly the reasons are obvious. We are not prescribing essential nutrients or their levels; we are simply feeding those whole raw foods the animal in question evolved to require.

No problem of harmful chemical reactions

The **fifth** principle is that given no cooking is involved, the components may be ground and mixed together with no problems of unwanted chemical reactions occurring between the components. This is food in its most health promoting form —aka what happens in nature.

Expert committee not required

The **sixth** principle is that this programme does not depend on the opinions of a committee of nutritional experts. It relies on feeding the scope and balance of the wide range of whole raw foods an animal evolved to eat.

No changes required

The **seventh** principle is that all the basic principles — as stated — remain valid and are not amenable to change. Therefore we can believe them and we can have total confidence in the foods that are developed using this set of principles.

No conflict between principles and feeding trials

The **eighth** principle is that these principles do not in any way conflict with any feeding trials that may be used to validate the food. Once again this totally contrasts with the fake industrial food program.

Legally AND biologically complete and balanced

The **ninth** principle is that these raw foods will be both legally and biologically complete and balanced. Legally, because they will pass the AAFCO feeding trials and biologically complete and balanced because RAW supplies the nutrients we do know to be essential and also those essential nutrients not as yet discovered, or not as yet discovered to be essential — e.g. phytonutrients. This is the only nutritional program that can claim to be truly complete and balanced.

EVOLUTIONARY NUTRITION — BOTTOM LINE

All nutrients present

The bottom line is that by feeding RAW — the entire nutritional requirements of that animal are met.

No training

This will be accomplished without having to understand any modern nutritional science whatsoever.

Whole raw foods

Eating whole raw foods is how our dogs and cats have survived and thrived prior to the advent of processed pet foods. It was in fact, healthy long-lived dogs and cats eating their whole raw foods that taught me about evolutionary nutrition in the early part of my veterinary career.

Evolutionary nutrition – it's the Gold Standard!

Clearly, evolutionary nutrition is the gold standard way to feed our dogs. Other equally apt terms include natural diet and species appropriate diet.

All others – of lower standard

Any other diet, is by definition of a lower standard and therefore less likely to promote good health. The evolutionary Diet allows animals to reach their genetic potential in terms of health, longevity, physical activity and reproduction [if required] The further an animal's diet departs from its evolutionary diet, the more health problems that animal is likely to develop.

Truth makes compliance easy

Once this profound nutritional truth is understood and accepted, it becomes very easy for pet owners to want to feed, and for health professionals to want to recommend, an evolutionary diet for pet animals. Producing this understanding is another matter. As my mother was fond of saying — "There are non-so-blind as those who will not see".

EVOLUTIONARY FOOD – EASY TO PRODUCE

So, how do we produce an evolutionary or RAW diet for our dogs and cats?

Use whatever you can acquire (beg, borrow, buy, or find) in the way of whole raw healthy foodstuffs – meat, bones, vegetables and organ meats etc. – that mimics the diet of a wild or feral animal.

Most, if not all of these products may be found at your local supermarket. The programme may also include eggs, milk products and other healthy human foods.

It may also include supplements such as vitamins, essential fatty acids, probiotics, kelp, alfalfa powder, various herbs etc. These replace the faeces and soil and other materials that a dog in nature would consume.

These principles are outlined in "Give Your Dog a Bone", "The BARF Diet", "Grow Your Pups with Bones" and "Pointing the Bone at Cancer."

Once the principles of evolutionary nutrition are understood, finding the components and feeding the program becomes uniquely simple.

SUMMARISING THIS AAFCO VS RAW FOOD DISCUSSION

1. AAFCO standards — mostly guesses and subject to change

Because the AAFCO standards are based on compromises and guesses and on foods that are biologically inappropriate as food for dogs or cats, it is not possible to place any reliance on such nutritional standards.

2. AAFCO standards — as outlined in their guidebook do not apply to raw whole foods

In other words, AAFCO standards have no role in the production of RAW foods for companion animals. If AAFCO standards apply to any type of food — it would only be fake industrial food. AAFCO standards are both irrelevant and misleading when constructing raw diets. The sub-standard ingredients used in FIF's in no way relate to the whole raw foods our dogs are designed by evolution to require and this is an issue that cannot be dismissed. It should also be noted … that AAFCO admits its irrelevance to raw whole foods!

3. AAFCO standards also irrelevant to fake industrial foods

Ironically — for all the reasons discussed — including most particularly that a successful feeding trial can make complete nonsense of the AAFCO written standards or rules — those AAFCO standards are also irrelevant and meaningless in terms of the production of fake industrial foods.

4. AAFCO feeding trials – a mixed blessing

And finally as we have seen the AAFCO feeding trials can best be described as a mixed blessing. On the negative side, they allow very poor examples of industrial dog foods to easily qualify as AAFCO compliant. On the positive side, raw food producers can use these trials to qualify their products, as AAFCO compliant and we know that veterinarians — will not argue with the result of an AAFCO feeding trial!

Evidence from my own dogs

Please note that every dog, I have ever owned has — in a sense — passed the AAFCO feeding trials. That is – apart from a period of two years, early in my veterinary career — each one of them has only ever eaten raw whole foods for all of its long and healthy life, has passed the vet exam, has passed the blood tests (and more) and has retained its weight. More importantly, it has rarely required my services – as a vet. Millions of RAW fed dogs around the world are also achieving the exact same pass.

THE OBVIOUS CONCLUSION — AAFCO RULES — GENERALLY OF NO VALUE

This should be of major concern to veterinarians

Given all of the above, we must conclude that the meaninglessness and virtual irrelevance of the AAFCO nutritional standards in relation to canine and feline nutrition applies whether we are talking about fake industrial foods (AAFCO's only genuine concern) or raw whole foods. From this we have to conclude that the reliance that vets and other canine health professionals place on these standards is misplaced entirely. Any conclusions based on these standards have to be viewed with not only enormous skepticism — but in fact — with absolute and complete mistrust.

The AAFCO guidelines are a heroic attempt by a group of so-called or would be "experts" — to produce regulations for producing nutritionally sound products from materials that barely deserve the word food to be appended to their names. This long-winded and complex attempt may be best described as a heroic failure. This is a set of rules, not only subject to constant change, but also — with its myriad disclaimers, modifications, qualifications and footnotes — meaningless as a definitive set of guidelines. A careful reading of this guide gives it away as being a collection of compromises, guesses and opinions… a fact that the writers admit, freely and without hesitation throughout the text.

Vets lack understanding

None of this is appreciated by today's veterinary profession; all they "know" — *or think they know* — is that there exists — this definitive set of guidelines written in stone and with all the imprimatur of holy writ. They have this view because this is what they were taught as students. They have this belief because it is the common belief within the profession. I would be prepared to guess that very few to no vets in companion animals practice would have read this book. They simply believe — what they are told about these guidelines — and their definitive importance — by their nutritional teachers. I would also guess, that these teachers — who for the most part, are paid by or in some way beholden to the major pet food manufacturers — may also never have read — in any detail — or at all in most cases — this complex set of rules. They too, simply believe the spin and rhetoric dished up by their masters.

Let me note that — YES — I have been severely critical of the AAFCO Guidelines. The point that I am making is that the AAFCO set of guiding principles is not and should not be seen by anyone — including most particularly the veterinary profession — as any sort of authority in terms of canine or feline nutrition.

Complex industrial rules vs simplicity of raw

The way to view the complex set(s) of rules and regulations surrounding the use of the commonly used materials in fake industrial foods is to see them as an attempt to overcome the difficulties encountered by anyone trying to produce a nutritionally complete and balanced pet food from extremely inappropriate materials. The complexity of these rules is in stark contrast to the simplicity of using biologically appropriate raw materials.

WHAT CAN WE DO AS A COMMUNITY OF RAW FEEDERS?

Participate in the feeding trials

I would urge every maker of raw pet foods to take their products and sit the AAFCO feeding trials. Forget the analytical method. It is virtually worthless. Properly constructed RAW will pass the feeding trials with flying colours. And given the veterinary profession holds the AAFCO feeding trials in such high esteem or reverence, this will be one of the most meaningful things the raw-feeding community can do to explain the value of raw whole foods to the veterinary profession.

Visit your vet with healthy dogs

And of course those of you who do feed one of these raw products — with the AAFCO seal of approval — make this known to your vet. Take your dogs in for check-ups and blood work. We need our vets to learn the truth about raw feeding.

We need blood-work – a data-base

We also need to establish a database for normal blood-work based on dogs fed exclusively according to the principles of evolutionary nutrition.

Veterinary post-graduate training – its up to you!

Finally, it is vital that we use the available scientific resourced — veterinary examinations, blood-work etc. — to demonstrate — to ourselves — and others — including most particularly our vets — the health promoting attributes of properly constructed raw.

If you are a RAW feeder, I urge you to do this because post-graduate veterinary nutritional education lies in the hands of the raw feeders; I have seen this work; it is only the raw feeders themselves who can begin the education of our vets on this vital topic.

Copyright © Ian Billinghurst

www.drianbillinghurst.com

Natural Breeders Register

If you are looking for a new pet, or to re-home a pet, but want it to have come from or go to a raw feeding, non-chemically treated source, then try the Natural Breeders Register.

Facebook.com/groups/
NaturalBreedersRegisterUK

Copy Dates - 2017-2018

31st October 2017

31st January 2018

30th April 2018

31st July 2018

All articles, letters to the editor and fully formatted adverts are to be submitted at no later than the above dates for each next edition.

Send attached articles, photographs and .pdfs to :

contact@healthful.uk.com

Recommended Natural Therapists

Some therapies that we have investigated are certainly worth bearing in mind when certain circumstances arise with your pet. However due to a number of unethical, untrained, cowboys out there, that may not help your pet one bit and could potentially even make them worse, we recommend finding a practitioner via an association or regulatory body. Here are some of the therapies and associated regulatory bodies we recommend:

Acupuncture	www.abva.co.uk
Bowen	www.bowen-technique.com
Herbalist	www.herbalvets.org.uk www.vbma.org
Homeopathy	www.bahvs.com www.ahvma.org
Hydrotherapy	www.narch.org.uk
McTimoney	www.mctimoney-animal.org.uk
Physiotherapy	www.acpat.org
Reiki	www.reikifed.co.uk
Tellington Touch	www.ttouchteam.co.uk

Also any ANNAHP Registered therapist and all Wagdale practitioners.

www.annahp.co.uk   www.wagdale.org.uk

![Happy Paws ...WITH SUE]

Grooming with trust

Sue Williamson

Imagine if you can! Your partner pops you in the car, drives you to a strange place, passes you over to a strange lady who speaks a different language, then leaves you. You are surrounded by new smells, sights, noises and other people who are there crying and shouting, all in cages. Then you get dragged by the strange lady who makes you get on a high table and starts combing and cutting your hair and nails, and makes you have a bath!   Sounds scary!!! Well, this is what our dogs have to endure every time they go to the groomers. They have no idea what is happening, have no control of what is being done, and any communication they are trying to make is being ignored, whether it is pulling their paw away from nails being clipped, snapping at clippers or howling at the top of their voice!

Now imagine, that instead of the communication being ignored, the strange lady listens to you. When the dog pulls his paw away, she lets it go. When you start looking away from her, she stops what she is doing, and when you just want to lie down and enjoy your pampering, she lets you! Doesn't that sound more relaxing for both the dog and the groomer?

I know what I would prefer, and as a Tellington TTouch Training (TTouch) [1] Practitioner (P1), Trust is at the centre of my methodology for grooming dogs. I want the dogs to know that they can be confident that I am not going to hurt them. I have learnt that dogs cope much better with grooming if they are able to communicate what they are comfortable with, and what they do not like, and that I will listen and act accordingly. Most people now insist on positive training methods, so why should it be any different for grooming?

Sarah Fisher talks about thinking in terms of a dog having a bank account (April 2017. Positive actions are deposits (eg. Treats, playing) whilst negative actions are withdrawals (negative grooming, vets, punishment, etc). We always need to ensure that we deposit more than we withdraw to ensure the dogs bank account is always in credit. Grooming can be a massive withdrawal for a dog, which means that it leaves the salon in a worse position than it entered, resulting in the dog starting the next visit to the groomers already with much lower credit than the start of the previous groom.

Working with the dog, rather than "on" the dog", giving it lots of opportunity to "communicate" what it does and doesn't like, means that the dog leaves the salon with a much wealthier bank account than using force to get through the groom. The dog is happier and the groomer less stressed.

Case Study - Millie

Millie is a cream 7 month old Cockerpoo who had never been groomed before. She came in with her terrier cross sister, so she had something familiar in the salon with her. Unfortunately, like many Cockerpoos, the owner had found it difficult to maintain a mat free coat, and although not severely matted I decided that her coat was too matted to brush out without causing distress.

During this first visit to me, she made it very clear to me that she didn't like any part of the grooming process, including the clippers and drier. She panicked immediately they were switched on. As Mandy Petit (July 2017) states

"Behavior is the only way our animals can

communicate with us"

So in response to "listening" to her concerns instead of continuing with the clippers, I scissored out the thickest mats on her torso and legs, leaving her quite patchy. She did not enjoy the bath, but coped better as I did some TTouch work and allowed her to wrap her front legs around my arm.

She also hated the dryer, so as it was a warm day, and I still had her sister to groom, I patted down her coat with a towel and let her dry naturally.

During the process of the groom, I knew that I had made bank withdrawals so needed to do something to put the account back into credit before she left me. As I have a miniature poodle who is extremely calm in the grooming salon, and I had permission from the owner, I allowed them supervised play for a short while, then ensured I gave Millie lots of fuss before she left.

On collection, the owner agreed to weekly visits until I was able to positively familiarise Millie with the whole process.

On Millie's second visit, she came into the salon in front of her owner, tail wagging, came directly to me and allowed me to stroke her. This confirmed to me that I had given her a mainly positive experience on her first visit to me. However, we still needed to help her to overcome her fear of the grooming process.

Once the owner had left, I settled Millie on the table with a treat seeking mat (2) with treats, and whilst she was searching and eating treats I scissored off the remaining coat on her torso. I was also able to scissor a little off around her face following her lead on when she was happy for me to do so. If she sat

still, I snipped away, as soon as she started moving her head I stopped. As I wanted this visit to be very positive, that is all I did. When the owner returned, I demonstrated the training element of Chirag Patel's Bucket Game (28/3/2017). I asked the owner to continue with the training in preparation for the following week.

During the week, the owner had "charged" the bucket, so after a few repeats of charging on the third visit, whilst playing the game, I started to use the clippers on Millie to tidy up the coat. Whilst she looked at the bucket, still being rewarded with a treat, I switched on the clippers and watched her reaction. She continued to look at the bucket, so I moved the clippers nearer until I touched her body with the body of the clippers so she could feel the vibration, she disengaged with the bucket, so I stopped. Once she re-engaged I continued with stroking her with the clippers, this time she remained engaged with the bucket, so I continued and then turned the clipped so I was clipping the fur. She had quickly learned that she could trust me with the clippers!

She also needed a bath, so as she had done so well with the clippers, I gave her a little play time with Chic, whilst I got the bath ready. As I had already deposited a lot of trust, Millie was much better in the bath, so I was able to do this really quickly, using a little TTouch.

Back on the table, we returned to the bucket game as I switched on the dryer at a distance from her. Moving it closer as she was interacting with the game. After a few minutes, the dryer was directly above her, and she was shoving her face upwards towards the dryer and keeping it there. This was no longer a dog that disliked the dryer!!!

The owner was shown how to use the bucket game so that she could start to groom Millie properly at home to prevent future matting, and build trust with the owner.

Giving Millie an element of control over the groom using the bucket game, quickly built up the trust between us. Ensuring that Millie received more positive experiences (bank deposits) then negative ones (withdrawals) has resulted in Millie no longer being afraid of being groomed.

Millie now runs into my gate then salon, and is a joy to groom.

During the year I have been grooming on my own, using these gentle trust based techniques I have found that both the dog and myself are less stressed and that the groom actually doesn't take much longer than using the force method.

The trust starts as soon as the dog walks in my gate, I follow the dogs lead. If they want to come and say hello (which many of my regulars do with waggy tails), then I will fuss them, those who are a little more reserved I leave alone whilst I discuss requirements with the owner. If I need to hold the dog whilst the owner leaves, I always get the owner to pick up the dog and pass to me, much more reassuring for the dog!

When owner has left, I do a quick observation of the dog to assess how it is feeling and whether it needs a little time to adjust to the salon before pushing ahead with the groom. I am very conscious that the dog, especially for their first groom with me, is in a new environment, new smells, sights, person, equipment, etc., and that they need to adjust to this and be comfortable. Pushing ahead before the dog has had time to acclimatise can be yet another trigger.

Once on the table, I don't immediately start the groom, I will spend a little time stroking the dogs, perhaps using Tellington TTouch Training body work, getting a feel of the dog, any areas the dog may not be comfortable to be touched, hot or cold spots

(which can indicate potential tension, injury or sore area) etc. Then I can make a plan of how to proceed with the groom.

Although I use restraints, these are only used for safety purposes so that dog cannot fall off the table, they are not used to hold the dog still. Many of my dogs prefer to lay down whilst being dried for example, which is fine by me, I just work around them, just getting them to stand to dry underneath.

My aim for the future is to bring this positive method of grooming dogs to the wider grooming community. Using these methods, in my experience, does not extend the time it takes to groom the dog. Instead of certain aspects taking lots of time, eg. clipping nails when the dog is snatching the paw away constantly, building up trust means that nails can be clipped quickly and safely. I will be delivering my first workshop to groomers in November 2017 and happy to say the take up has been excellent.

[1] Tellington TTouch Training is a gentle way of working with animals using bodywork, ground work and specific equipment to help with physical, mental and emotional issues.

[2] A treat seeking mat is an enrichment toy which encourages dogs to use their noise and brain, but can also be used to distract a dog whilst grooming.

HTTP: WWW.HAPPYPAWSWITHSUE.CO.UK

References:

Fisher, S (2017) Tellington TTouch Training Practitioners Workshop, Tilley Farm Bath, April 2017

Petitt, M (2017) Tellington TTouch World (Facebook) 8.7.2017. Available from www.facebook.com [Accessed 08/07/2017]

Patel C, *Giving Dog Training Back to the Dogs: Empowering the Canine Learner Seminar*, Peterborough 28/3/2017

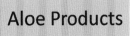

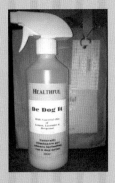

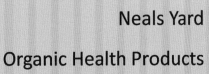

The Yorkshire Essence Flower Trials

Caroline Thomas

I approach this article with the understanding that you know nothing about what Flower Essences are and do. Flower Essences are Vibrational Medicines, which is based on the scientific principles that all matter vibrates to a precise frequency and that by using resonant vibration, balance of matter can be restored. Almost everything around, us has a living pulse inside of it, which vibrates at its own unique frequency. Flower Essences work on the principle that like attracts like. The different parts of your dog's physical, emotional, mental and spiritual being resonate to various frequencies of vibration. If your dog is depressed, he will be resonating at a lower frequency but by giving him a Flower Essence such as 'Gorse' which resonates at a higher frequency, it will raise his vibration and the depression will gently lift and a new layer of happiness will appear. The most commonly known range of Flower Essences are the Bach Flowers, which were created by Edward Bach during the last Century. He cleverly fashioned a way of harnessing the energy of the flower with the dew of the rain and the power of the sun. They are so different from herbal medicine, as each Flower Essence ONLY contains the energy of the flower and NO part of the plant. This makes Flower Essences 100% safe to use with conventional vet medicine and any other therapies that maybe needed.

After Edward Bach created his range of Flower Essences, many others were inspired by his work to create their own ranges. In May 2016, I was very fortunate to be able to meet with Rebecca and Chris from the Bailey Essences in Ilkley. Chris is the wife of Arthur Bailey, who was the founder of the Bailey Essences and Rebecca, his beloved step daughter. They had kept the name of the Bailey Essences going since Arthur passed away a few years before. I had been writing a book for them about how the Bailey Essences can help animals with emotional problems. This was the very first-time meeting in person, after many years of emails. Ilkley, is a very beautiful spa town and nestles next to the Moors.

This was a time when the Bailey Essences, had decided to change ownership, as Rebecca was living in Canada and it was becoming increasingly difficult to manage the Flower Essences Business from so far away. It was a decision that was not taken lightly and it needed to be someone who was known to Chris and Rebecca. Jenny Howarth had known the Bailey family for some time and was a Flower Essence Producer herself, so it made logical sense that she could take over. As this was a huge undertaking, Jenny asked Nicky Whitehead to help and it was here that the Yorkshire Essences were born.

On this momentous meeting, I was very nervous as had been writing my book for around 3 years and was worried that Jenny and Nicky would not have quite the same passion as Rebecca had about the book. I was so pleased when they too shared the same enthusiasm that I did, so I could actually finish writing the final chapters.

I spoke to Jenny and Nicky at length about developing a range of essences for animals, as I was becoming increasingly more aware of the mental health issues that were presenting in our dogs. On a daily basis I was receiving emails from owners who needed help with their dogs who were suffering from anxiety, depression, stress and typical OCD behaviours. It was obvious to me that animals as in many cases were mirroring the human world. In crisis as humans we often turn to anti-depressants to help solve our own insecurities. As a Registered Pharmacy Technician, I work with anti-depressants daily and they do have their place in our civilisation as they allow people to return to work, hold down jobs and function as best they can, in an increasingly busy, stressful society but Flower Essences can also do the same too.

Having trained with the Bach Flower Centre and the Natural Animal Centre, I understood how Flower Essences worked and understood also basic animal behaviour. I worked out from very early on that if the evolutionary needs of the dog were not being met, it was here that the problem was born. For example, not being socialised to as many stimuli as possible during the 'socialisation period' which is usually around 7 to 12 weeks. Dogs are often collected from the breeder at around 8 weeks of age, so this period is a critical window of opportunity to introduce your puppy to 'EVERYTHING'. The problems arise when the socialisation period is missed for some reason and the experiences that could have been learnt have been lost. This could be due to a myriad of differing personal intentions of trying to do the best by your dog but just not having the time.

The first thing I had to do was to work out what behaviours were in most need of being helped by Flower Essences. It did not take me long to work out these conditions, as they were being emailed to me daily by owners who were at their wits ends. These were the dogs literally living on their nerves, in a constant state of fear and anxiety.

1. Space/Fear Aggression

2. Socialisation

3. Liberation

4. Grief

5. Fears

6. Separation Anxiety

7. Transition

I spent the summer of 2016 drawing inspiration from the flowers in my garden and the work of Arthur Bailey. As the summer ended I had created the recipes for the 7 combination essences listed above, using the Yorkshire Essence range. With the help of some of the students from my Hoof and Paw Academy. The first thing that I needed to do was to meet up with Mandy and Paula who lived close by, so that we could come up with a plan of action. Mandy designed the feedback forms and we discussed what type of information we needed, such as vet permission, description of the problem, a list of animal behaviours and so much more. I put out an advert on my Hoof and Paw Facebook page and was overwhelmed by the amount of interest and the commitment of people who wanted to trial one of the composite essences. This was further proof that animals were suffering emotionally. Each animal was then categorised as to which trial they would be in and the coordinator of the trial then contacted the owner and it was here that relationships started to be formed. The three of us met often and during one of those meetings we made up the seven composite essences, asked for Arthur Bailey's inspiration and created a spiritual environment of love and positivity. Each composite was carefully packaged with instructions, stock bottle and treatment bottle and then posted to locations dotted all over the world. The trials lasted for 12 weeks and the feedback forms were returned with almost a 100% success rate. The data is still being processed and will be written up into a scientific paper, which will be shared in the future with vets and animal behaviourists.

The Scintilla Essences can be purchased from the Yorkshire Essence Website.

www.emotionalhealing4animals.co.uk   https://www.facebook.com/caroline382/
https://www.yorkshirefloweressences.com/products/scintilla-set-for-animals

ANNAHP AWARDS 2017

Celebrating Healthful Dogs' Third Anniversary we have teamed up with ANNAHP to organise awards for our incredible contributors. You voted for the best articles in each category.

Here are the results:

Best Holistic Therapy Article

Mary Debono

Debono Moves
Senior Dog with Spinal Arthritis Walks Easily Again.
Healthful Dog 3[3]:184-187

Best Food Article

Jodie Gruenstern

Mushroom Mystery Solved! Why are Mushrooms so Miraculous for Our Pets?
Healthful Dog 4[2]:86-91

Best Health Article

Deva Khalsa

The Allergy Epidemic.
Healthful Dog 3[3]:158-159

Most Interesting Article

Catherine O'Driscoll

Canine Health Concern
Vaccines and Mitochondrial Disease
Healthful Dog 3[4]:306-307

Most Helpful Article

H B Turner

Spotlight on Ethyl vs Methyl Mercury
Healthful Dog 4[1]:56-57

Thank you for voting

www.annahp.co.uk

I'm a Puppy Mummy

I'm a Puppy Mummy is an animal welfare campaign designed to ensure that should an emergency occur, your pets will be looked after, due to 'Pet Emergency Contact' details on a card in your purse or wallet.

Should an emergency occur, where you cannot get back to your animals, have a card on your person; this will prompt a call to your nominated 'Pet Emergency Contact', who will organise cover for your animal(s) whilst you are incapacitated.

To join this great scheme please go to :

www.imapuppymummy.com

VOSS Pets is a campaign to promote Vasectomies & Ovary Sparing Spays.

You as a pet owner have most likely done your research and found that <u>Spaying and Neutering reduces life span</u> but do not wish to risk contributing to the burgeoning number of un-wanted pets currently clogging up rescue centres & being put-to-sleep for no good reason; let alone the risk of spreading FIV (Feline Immunodeficiency Virus) or Canine Transmissible Cancer.

Vasectomies & Ovary Sparing Spays leave the hormones intact so that they can still perform their other functions, essential for your pets health.

Website: https://vosspets.wordpress.com/

Facebook: https://www.facebook.com/VOSSPets/

Donate: https://www.gofundme.com/v6tdspnm

Owner Odyssey
Death by Vaccinosis

Kes Stephenzon

Below is a basic outline of what happened to my Kodi and the events that led to his death. If his story can help other dogs, then at least I'll know he didn't die for nothing. Thank you for wishing to tell his story.

I'm going to start with Kodi's treatment at 6 weeks before his death as I don't know exactly what is significant.

Kodi had routine bloods done as he was a bit off colour and just not behaving as usual, he was a bit nervous and jumpy and had developed a bit of a cough. They took blood from his neck and obviously shaved a patch. His bloods all came back normal, his kidney and liver function in the normal range, nothing at all was cause for concern.

Two weeks later, I noticed that his hair had not even started to grow back in, and given thyroid problems run in my family, it made me suspect that this might be Kodi's problem too. He had more bloods and yes, his thyroid function was low, also after listening to his heart, they had detected a slight murmur but the vet did not feel it was particularly problematic at that time, to which I agreed and so it was agreed to just monitor it.

They started Kodi on thyroxin and tested his bloods again two weeks later to check his levels. His thyroid function was slightly high, I was told that was fairly normal for a dog taking thyroxin and so decided the dose was right. Again, his kidney and liver function was in the normal range, his heart had not deteriorated.

A few days later, he was due his check up and booster shots. At the time, my Gran was critically ill and so I was expecting Kodi to need to go to kennels in the near future. I was a little concerned, because I had never had a dog vaccinated before that had had health issues so discussed this with the vet. She didn't feel his booster would affect these and so I went ahead and had him done.

A few hours later, I noticed that Kodi was staggering slightly, this became worse during the night and so I phoned the vet. The vet said that yes it could be an effect of the booster, to keep an eye on him and to take him in the next day if he was no better.

By the following day, Kodi was finding it difficult to walk and to stand, he was leaning on the wall when trying to stand, and was unable to do his "needs" because his back end was so weak. His posture was very hunched also and he didn't want to eat. I took him back to the vet, where they admitted him both for observation and because they felt he needed to be immobilised in case of spinal injury.

They treated him with fluids as far as I'm aware, I didn't go see him for several days as he had become so stressed when I'd been in before. The vet said that she felt Kodi was improving but because his spinal X-ray had shown a defect, she wished to keep him immobilised and send his X-rays to the specialist in Stirling. The specialist agreed to see Kodi as an emergency case, but Kodi's vet phoned me and told me she didn't feel he needed to go as an emergency as his condition had improved. I hadn't seen him at that point so I took her word for it.

Later that day I felt I really wanted to see my dog and so I went in. When I saw Kodi I was devastated, he had clearly declined greatly since being admitted, he could hardly stand or walk, he had lost masses of weight and it was only then that I was told he had not eaten anything since being admitted, they believed this was because he was in pain and missing me. The vet on duty listened to my concerns and agreed that Kodi really should be sent as an emergency to the specialist as soon as possible. The day was Saturday, the soon as possible was Tuesday morning. Because the specialist was a 3 hour drive and I would need to leave before the vet opened, they agreed to let me take Kodi home on Monday night.

To be perfectly honest, that night, I knew he was seriously ill and I began to think that I would lose him.

Kodi who had been a very active, playful dog, was completely lifeless. He just lay on the floor, he wasn't interested in anything, not food, not the other dogs, nothing. He was totally drained. I took him to the specialist the next morning, the examination did not go very far however because after I explained Kodi's behaviour and rapid decline, the specialist suspected renal failure despite his bloods having been clear only a few days previously.

The bloods confirmed that Kodi's kidneys were barely functional at the time of testing, they also admitted him to their ICU ward and to give them credit, they worked around the clock to try to save him, sadly when the bloods were repeated his kidneys showed no sign of improvement at all and his other body organs were starting to shut down.

They let me take Kodi home that night, they gave him pain meds and steroids to try to keep him reasonably comfortable for the journey home and he was to be euthanised the following day.

Euthanasia was extremely difficult, Kodi's body was so shut down that they could not get a vein to inject.

They managed to get a tiny amount of the drug in and Kodi finally passed away around an hour later.

You can probably see why it was concluded to be his vaccinations that did the damage as he had been in almost perfect health, no kidney or liver issues as was shown by his bloods only days before the booster.

His decline happened only hours after the booster and within days, his body just gave up. Neither the vet practise or the specialist were able to come up with any other explanation to why Kodi just crashed as he did and at no time did they seem to even consider it to be anything other than his booster that caused his illness and death.

The vet was very open with me and even stated that she felt she had made mistakes as regards Kodi's care. She admitted that she should not have delayed his specialist appointment without my first seeing Kodi, however the specialist didn't believe it would have made any difference, Kodi would have died anyway, once his organs had started to give up, there was no reversing it, it was too quick and to be honest, I agree with that.

The only thing that might have saved him was not to vaccinate him and I wish I had known then what I know now. My instincts at the time were to not vaccinate, but I was at a loss as to what else I could do, given he would need to go to kennels.

As it turned out, he died and my gran died the very next day. So really, I put my boy through that for nothing I was there for neither of them in the end up and that kills me every day.

I don't blame Kodi's vet, I don't believe she vaccinated him just for the money, I believe she honestly thought it was what was best. I do believe that she should possibly have looked for advice, given Kodi's medical history and that's why I think education is the key. I know she has learnt some important lessons from what happened to Kodi and I also know she was genuinely devastated.

Debono Moves

A Terrier's Holistic Recovery from Hip Surgery

By Mary Debono, GCFP

Zoey

When Natalie was told that her three-year-old dog needed hip surgery, she was devastated. She wondered if her little terrier mix, Zoey, would ever be able to run, play and chase squirrels after femoral head ostectomy (FHO) surgery. After being assured by her veterinarian and other experts that small dogs do especially well with this hip surgery, Natalie began to breathe easier. Everyone she consulted told Natalie that her canine companion would be running around again in no time!

After more than three months post-surgery, the terrier still wouldn't use her leg.

But that was not the case with Zoey. While many vets say that dogs should be weight bearing two to three weeks after FHO surgery, Zoey was still not standing on her leg after three *months*!

Worse, the dog's leg was stiff and her muscles were atrophied. Natalie, an experienced physical therapist, did rehabilitation exercises with her dog. She also took Zoey to swim therapy (canine hydrotherapy), which was very helpful in exercising Zoey's repaired hip. But no matter what approach was tried, the little terrier still wouldn't use her leg on land.

This was troubling. For one thing, Zoey was dangerously stressing her opposite leg and back. In addition, weight-bearing activities that build muscle are critical to the success of FHO surgery. Since there is no longer a true hip joint, the muscles around the hip needed to be strengthened so that they could support Zoey's femur. For the little tan terrier to live a healthy, active life, she needed to start using that leg!

Could the *Feldenkrais Method®* be the key to the dog's recovery?

As time marched on, Natalie was becoming increasingly frustrated and stressed over her little dog's inability to recover. Then fate intervened.

Three months after Zoey's FHO surgery, I was in Los Angeles giving a presentation on how the *Feldenkrais Method®* helps humans and dogs move more easily despite injury, surgery, arthritis, anxiety and aging. Natalie happened to be in the audience. She contacted me after my presentation and I suggested that she check out my book, Grow Young with Your Dog.

Shortly after Natalie did *Connected Breathing* with Zoey, the little terrier began using her leg.

One of the first exercises that I teach people is how to use their breath and attention to connect deeply

The names of the individuals in this story, including the Akita, have been changed.

with their dog. I call this exercise *Connected Breathing*. This simple, yet powerful technique not only relaxes human and dog, but it can build an amazing bond.

Shortly after Natalie did *Connected Breathing* with Zoey, the little terrier began using and trusting her leg. After that exciting accomplishment, Natalie progressed to more of the hands-on techniques and exercises from my book to further improve her dog's body awareness and movement.

Now that Zoey was using her leg, Natalie could take her for longer walks and incorporate other muscle-strengthening activities into her life. In no time at all, the little tan dog was running and playing normally. She even started chasing squirrels again!

To keep her dog happy and healthy, Natalie continues to do my hands-on techniques and exercises, especially when Zoey has had a very active day. Natalie enjoys the stress-reducing benefits that the exercises have on her too.

All that is wonderful news, but it may have left you with some questions. For example: *How in the world did a calming, breathing exercise help Zoey use her leg?*

After a major injury or surgery, the body often goes into a fearful, protective state

When a major injury, surgery or emotional trauma is experienced, the individual may go into a fearful, protective state. The characteristics of this state include movement limitations, stiffness, discomfort, anxiety, guarding and holding onto harmful movements or inappropriate behaviors. A dog in a fearful-protective state may exhibit one or more of these attributes.

For a full recovery, dogs need to be in a confident, connected state

For a full recovery, dogs need to be in a confident, connected state. Dogs in a confident-connected state are usually receptive to exploring and learning new things. They are comfortable, curious and connected with others.

The dog's nervous system was still dealing with the trauma of the hip surgery

Three months after her FHO surgery, Zoey was still stuck in a fearful-protective state. It's important to point out that the little terrier continued to be friendly and charming during this time. Other than not wanting to stand on her leg, she didn't appear fearful or protective. But below the surface, Zoey's nervous system was still dealing with the trauma of the hip surgery. This prevented her from gaining the confidence to use her repaired leg.

Health is achieved by gently guiding our dogs into a confident-connected state

For Zoey to fully recover, Natalie first needed to "reset" or calm her dog's nervous system. And *Connected Breathing* was an effective, pleasurable way to do that.

Calming the terrier's nervous system allowed her to move from a fearful-protective state to a confident-connected state. This change can affect a dog's physiology and behavior in a myriad of positive ways.

Calming the nervous system sets the stage for improvement to occur. The dog breathes easier. Anxiety dissipates. The dog realizes that it's possible to feel differently. The vicious cycle has been interrupted.

Once she was in a confident-connected state, Zoey's brain registered that her leg could support weight. She started using her leg almost immediately.

Zoey's journey to full recovery is a wonderful example of how canine health is not achieved by treating parts of a body, but by gently guiding our dogs into a confident-connected state. In other words, a *holistic* recovery.

Click here to watch a video of Zoey happily digging, spinning and playing after her recovery from FHO surgery. It's nice to see her having so much fun!

Learn how to do *Connected Breathing* with your dog

Click here for both text and audio instructions so you can do *Connected Breathing* with your dog. Your dog doesn't have to be recovering from an injury or surgery for *Connected Breathing* to be beneficial to your dog's well-being. In addition to being a way to deepen the canine-human bond, it can be a great stress-reliever for you too!

What is Femoral Head Ostectomy (FHO) Surgery?

To understand FHO surgery, it's helpful to know the parts of the hip. The hip joint is a ball-and-socket joint. The ball part is the *head* of the dog's thigh bone (*femur*). The ball sits on a stem, which is called the *neck*. The ball fits into the hip socket (*acetabulum*), which is a concave portion of the dog's pelvis.

In a FHO, the surgeon removes the "ball" and

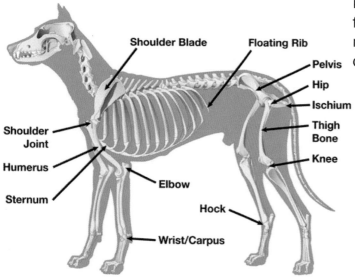

"stem" parts of the ball-and-socket hip joint.

In a FHO, the surgeon removes the head and neck of the dog's femur (thigh bone). In other words, the "ball" and "stem" parts of this ball-and-socket joint are taken off. With these parts gone, the dog's thigh

bone no longer touches the hip socket. This can eliminate the pain that was caused by the bones of the hip joint abnormally contacting each other. For dogs with chronically aching hips, a FHO can give them a chance at a pain-free life.

Many dogs, especially small ones, recover well from FHO surgery.

Although this orthopedic surgery sounds alarming, it's amazing how dogs can adapt to this radical change in their hip joints. During the healing process, the dog's body will produce scar tissue which creates a "false joint." In addition, the dog's hind-quarter muscles help hold the hip in place. Building strength in the repaired leg is vital for a full return to function. Fortunately, many dogs, especially small ones, recover well from FHO surgery.

FHO is usually recommended when a dog's hip cannot be repaired by any other means.

Femoral head ostectomy is used in cases of painful hip dysplasia and arthritis, as well as dislocated (luxated) and traumatized hips. Dogs diagnosed with Legg-Calvé-Perthes Disease may also be candidates for FHO surgery. Simply put, FHO is usually recommended when a dog's hip cannot be repaired by any other means.

Mary Debono is a *Guild Certified Feldenkrais Practitioner^cm* and the creator of the *Grow Young with Your Dog®* and *Grow Young with Your Horse^sm* programs. She is the author of the Amazon #1 best seller, *Grow Young with Your Dog,* which won the Best Health Book in the 2015 San Diego Book Awards.

In a career spanning more than 25 years, Mary has helped thousands of individuals, ranging from disabled dogs to high-performing equine and human athletes. Based in Encinitas, California, Mary travels internationally to teach people how to help animals and humans feel younger and more vital at any age.

To reach more people around the globe, Mary is now offering online consultations and courses. Her website is www.DebonoMoves.com

www.DebonoMoves.com

Cruciate Problems

Pennie Clayton

I would like to introduce myself, my name is Pennie Clayton I am a horse and dog trainer and a Bowen therapist. I treat humans, horses and dogs, and run I canine Bowen courses with a colleague. The introduction may be needed as I may make references to horses as well as dogs which sometimes puzzle people.

I love dogs, I am owned by two lurchers and one greyhound. The two lurchers are now approaching extreme old age, and have their individual health challenges, which means that their wellbeing and welfare takes up a lot of my thoughts. I think we can all sympathise with the fact that we would all like to know more about how to keep our animals healthy and that their welfare is top of the list of our priorities.

In my role of canine Bowen therapist I often come across dogs with cruciate ruptures, or suspected tears to the cruciate. I have found that Bowen is very helpful as part of the healing process, especially if owners are careful, follow vets instructions, and act on any suggestions that I may have.

The reason that cruciate problems sprang to mind when I was thinking about writing an article for Healthful dog is because they are so common.

Cruciate problems centre around the fact that the cruciate ligaments serve to stabilise the dogs patella (knee joint). If damage occurs in this area then the dog immediately exhibits symptoms, lameness and pain are classic symptoms of tears and damage to the cruciate ligament.

If an internet search is done on causes there are many suggestions but my research (admittedly much of which has been gathered on conversations with clients and observations during my travels) has lead me to conclude that people's skewed attitudes towards exercise is partly to blame. People are made to feel bad if they don't exercise their dogs. Exercise fulfils many functions but what it should not do is to lead to the damage and breakdown of a dogs' body.

Exercise has all kinds of meanings to many people. People often feel that slower walks do little to fulfil the daily exercise requirement and frown upon allowing their dogs time to sniff and ponder what they find as they wander around outside. Rather than allow a walk to take shape as the dog might choose they favour a lot of vigorous activity including chasing balls and using the ubiquitous "ball chuckers". Any activity that encourages dogs to run and jump further, and faster, seems to be encouraged and in vogue these days. As far as young dogs, and puppies, are concerned these kinds of activity can often result in damage and stress to many areas of the body with injuries and tears to the cruciate becoming very commonplace. The opposite leg often becomes damaged too if exercise is not modified after initial damage to one hind leg occurs.

Young dogs' bodies are fragile and the way they are exercised has a direct link to their health. Dogs' growth plates are not fully closed until a dog is over 16 months old. Inappropriate exercise especially that which is out of the normal range of movement can cause damage to the growing bones and skeleton. Jumping, turning and twisting for balls puts considerable pressure on the bones and tendons of the legs, especially as dogs tend to carry the majority of weight on their front legs. They are just not designed to take weight onto one hind leg as they jump or land awkwardly.

Other activities that can also cause ongoing damage are continuous running, playing without rests and being asked to jump in and out of a car (particularly on a cold day, or when the weather is hot and the dog is over heated after vigorous running) These everyday activities can all have an adverse effect on young bones as well as soft tissue of all types. If this is ongoing and continues into maturity then cruciate damage is very likely to occur. Relatively young dogs have been known to have cruciate damage which is horrifying, and unnecessary, but it is most common around 5-8 years of age.

Over exercise is not the only factor which increases the possibility of cruciate damage. Poor nutrition can also be a contributory factor, as can early neutering and spaying.

If a young dog grows too fast through incorrect feeding then more pressure is put on the skeleton and structures that surround it, storing up problems for later in life.

What still surprises me is that how few dogs have bodywork. All types of bodywork are very common in the horse world, a good therapist can often pick up areas of restriction and imbalance, that an owner is unaware of.

Dog owners are often unaware of how useful and integral bodywork could be for their own dogs. There are many therapies on offer and admittedly it can be confusing as to which therapy to choose. As a Bowen therapist I often need to explain what we do, and what a Bowen treatment involves. Quite simply Bowen is very gentle hands on physical therapy. It is non manipulative and we work on soft tissue. We do not use any harsh movements or force the dog to stay in one place as we treat them, which means that the dog can choose how much treatment he receives. We accept that we often have to educate owners to allow their dogs to go into another room, or to a quiet area after what looks to be minimal contact, but that is the beauty of Bowen. We do not need to provoke a reaction in the body by using a lot of insistent contact with the body. Bowen is in fact composed of contact with the body and then pauses in treatment which we refer to as breaks, so we are pleased if a dog puts their own breaks in, it saves us deciding when and where to allow the body to rest and process the treatment we are giving. In fact the breaks are one of the areas where Bowen differs to a lot of other physical treatments.

Returning to the subject of cruciate injuries if the owner follows the general vet advice to cease exercising their dog which allows time for the injury to heal there are several things which may still not be addressed by resting. As injury occurs then compensation follows pretty quickly as a coping strategy. In this case dogs often try to relieve the injured leg by shifting more weight onto the other "good leg".

Other consequences include the dog putting more weight onto the front legs and causing tension and discomfort in the neck, shoulders which sometimes radiates down either side of the spine. This can be detected by the presence of increased heat or hot spots.

If tension can be relieved in these areas then the dog will immediately experience a sense of relief and this allows him to relax, rest and sleep allowing healing to take place. Rebalancing the body, relieving tension, and boosting circulation are all areas that can be assisted with Bowen.

One of my recent clients has been a dog of 6 years that sustained possible cruciate damage. When I assessed him on my first visit his entire body and fascia were very tight and restricted and he had heat around his injured leg, along his spine and around both hips. He was very aware of his injured leg and instead of standing equally on all 4 legs he balanced on the tips of his toes on the injured leg and moved by crossing it underneath him.

After this initial assessment he had a short Bowen treatment and his owners reported that he slept soundly for the rest of the night. When I saw him on a second visit a week later he was more confident about standing on his injured leg and he was moving more evenly. He also had no heat in the areas that had been affected the week before. They had been very good about sticking rigidly to the no exercise rule and when I completed a third visit he was much happier and freer in his movement.

This is the kind of feedback that occurs after a few treatments but as much as I love going out to see clients I would rather education about exercise was more available.

Prevention and education are far better than playing catch up with a dog's health.

www.horseandhoundschool.co.uk

The Dog -Athlete is an Acupressure Hound

By Amy Snow and Nancy Zidonis,
founders of Tallgrass Animal Acupressure Institute

Drake is an amazing agility dog. He darts on to the course taking the triple bar in stride,

running smoothly and efficiently through the entire course with grace and confidence.

His timing, movements, and keen attention are impressive. Not a moment's hesitation dashing up and down the A-frame, over a double-oxer, through the chute, on to the pause table, then off again at top speed to the broad jump, and to weave the poles – the consummate dog athlete!

Drake's Welsh Border Collie lineage makes him the perfect candidate for agility, and at six-years old, he is desperately in need of consistent acupressure treatments. When Drake is running the course, he is so excited and his natural pain-reducers, endorphins, are flowing through his veins and he barely feels anything except his utter joy in what he is born to do. During his off-course time, his shoulders and hips are obviously sore. He gets up from a nap and seems stiff at first, and then stretches his limbs cautiously.

Agility, Frisbee, ball fetching, strenuous hiking and all the many games and sports we engage in with our dogs are good, healthy exercise when not done to excess. Even if these activities are not taken to an extreme, tendons can become irritated and inflamed, muscles stressed and sore. As the dog ages the likelihood of joints becoming arthritic is very high. These are the types of conditions we see in dogs leading active lifestyles.

Acupressure can help your dog be more comfortable and perform at his best. Over hundreds of years, acupressure has proven to help resolve many of the painful conditions we see in athletic dogs because it can:

- Strengthen muscles, tendons, joints, and bones

- Enhance mental clarity and calm required for focus

- Release natural cortisone to reduce swelling and inflammation

- Increase lubrication of the joints for better movement

- Release endorphins to increase energy and relieve pain

- Resolve injuries more quickly by increasing blood supply

- Balance energy to optimize the body's ability to perform.

Your dog will have a lot more fun if he feels good when he is running after a ball or simply jogging with you on the beach. We recommend two different acupressure treatments. The first is "Before Activity," which serves as a warm-up and gets his body ready for the additional stress of intense movement. These acupressure points are used to increase blood circulation and release endorphins that can enhance the dog's athletic ability and help build long-term endurance. Hold these points by placing the ball of your thumb at a 90-degree angle to the dog's body or you can place your middle finger on top of your index finger and press the point gently with the ball of your index finger. The Before Activity treatment should be give at least one-hour and no more than 12 hours prior to the anticipated activity.

The second treatment is the "After Activity" treatment, this session will help your dog relax, move lactic acid out of the muscles thus reducing potential soreness, and build long-term muscle, joint, and tendon strength needed to enhance stamina. Use the same point work techniques suggested for the Before Activity session above. The After Activity session can be performed as soon as your dog has cooled down and you can work calmly with your dog.

If your dog is showing signs of acute pain or distress, we encourage you to take him to your holistic veterinarian. Acupressure is an excellent resource and complement to your dog's healthcare since you can perform treatments yourself, but it is not a substitute for veterinary care.

Your dog will enjoy playing, running, jumping, weaving through poles – whatever your sport - much more if you help take good care of his body. Acupressure is safe, always available, drug-free, and dogs' love the touch of their special people.

Before Activity Acupressure Points

Points	Location
Yin Tang	Located on the ventral midline, slightly above the level of the eyes.
St 36	Located just lateral to the tibial crest on the lateral aspect of the hindleg.
GB 34	In a depression behind and below the head of the fibula, lateral side of hind leg.

############

Nancy Zidonis and Amy Snow are the authors of: ACU-DOG: a Guide to Canine Acupressure, ACU-CAT: A Guide to Feline Acupressure, and ACU-HORSE: A Guide to Equine Acupressure. They founded Tallgrass Publishers offering books, manuals, DVDs, Apps, and meridian charts. Tallgrass Animal Acupressure Institute provides a 300-hour hands-on and online training program worldwide. To contact them: web:

www.animalacupressure.com; email: Tallgrass@animalacupressure.com

www.animalacupressure.com

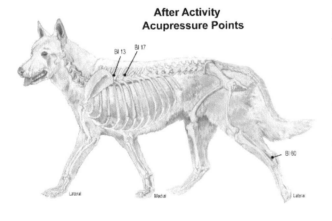

After Activity Acupressure Points

Points	Location
Bl 13	Located lateral to the spinous process of the 3rd thoracic vertebra.
Bl 17	Located lateral to the spinous process of the 7th thoracic vertebra.
Bl 60	Found on the lateral aspect of the hind leg, at the thinnest part of the hock.

Question Pet Food Ingredients

By Will Falconer

…As If Your Pet's Life Depended on It

Is this what your kibble is made of?

When you look at a colourful label on a pet food, do you believe the pictures represent what's really inside?

You may recall Dr. Randy Wysong is <u>suing several big players in the pet food industry</u>.

For exactly this issue of false advertising.

You know, steak and lamb chops on the outside and junk on the inside, nothing like what the pictures promised.

The companies are

- Nestle Purina Petcare
- Mars Petcare
- Wal-Mart
- Hills Pet Nutrition (who trained vet students, like me, in "nutrition." Ha!)
- BigHeart/J.M. Smucker
- Ainsworth/APN

Not surprisingly, they have all countered with a lame motion to dismiss.

Dr. Wysong's not buying it and neither should you.

Pet food ingredients are clearly not as manufacturers would have you believe.

Truth vs Bucks

Periodically, I pay <u>The Truth About Pet Food</u> a visit. Susan Thixton runs this site, and she's someone who's really dug into the pet food industry and isn't afraid to share the dirty truth of what's happening there.

Susan cited a great example of what you're up against as a pet food consumer recently.

Take a look at this image:

Nice looking cuts of meat there, right?

"Real Ingredients!" (what's that supposed to mean?)

"High quality ingredients?"

Here's another:

"Real Chicken?"

How bad could that be, real chicken?

But Susan always looks deeper, as a champion of pet owning consumers.

And she knows a thing or two about pet food ingredients.

Here she defines for you "food grade" vs "feed grade" and how both can be called "chicken."

It turns out the FDA watchdogs often look the other way and let condemned meat into pet food as "feed grade."

And the label can still call it "chicken" or "beef" and even out and out lie to you by calling it "human grade" when it's anything but.

That misrepresentation is exactly what Evangers did.

And they are still lying since the pentobarbital showed up in their supposedly "human grade" "100% Beef" canned goods, that killed at least one dog we know of.

A Grisly Reality

Stacey, a long time Pack member, wrote me shortly after I sent an issue of Vital Animal News with the Evanger's pentobarbital story.

Her detective work gives you a deeper sense of what you are up against if you trust pet food manufacturers:

When I went to the animal crematory to pick up our 18 yr old dogs ashes I saw something that was very upsetting. As I was exiting the business park here comes the San Jose Tallow truck swinging the corner....I flipped a U-turn and followed, parked across the street to watch...

He went to the crematory, backed his truck up to the back of the crematory truck (it was a Monday-they pick up from the vets offices on Mondays around our town) and they proceeded to toss the black bags to the tallow driver and emptied a couple of bins then moved 2, 55 gallon drums with a dolly onto the tallow truck as well. I was horrified.

While tallow is, strictly speaking, animal fat from rendered animals, the take away here is that pets, perhaps euthanized at the end of their lives, can and do end up as pet food ingredients.

And the crematorium is complicit in this, and lying to you in their own way.

Whose ashes were you actually given?

Why it's Critical to Be a Critical Thinker

Perhaps now, as never before in history, it pays for you to be wise.

Especially so when you are caring for a defenceless animal, who eats what ever you offer, takes treatments or prevention that you deem as helpful, and lives a vital or devitalized life depending on the wisdom of your choices.

- Taking pet food labels (or crematorium promises) at face value is unwise.

As is accepting the idea that annual vaccination is <u>necessary</u> or even <u>good for your animal</u>.

As is trusting that internal pesticide feeding (for <u>heartworm "prevention"</u> or <u>flea control</u>) is the most acceptable option.

Let us know in the comments if you are warier this year than you were 3-5 years ago.

Tell us if you're making homemade food and if so, what are your recipe origins.

And further, what are your trusted sources of information? I hope discovering Susan's work on pet food has been a help to you.

About Will Falconer, DVM

Homeopathic veterinarian and teacher of animal people. Learn how to make smart choices to raise truly Vital Animals.

http://vitalanimal.com/

NURTURE THEM NATURALLY

RAW FOOD SPECIALISTS

2 DARTMOUTH COURT, GOSPORT, HAMPSHIRE, PO14 4EW 02392 177271

NURTURETHEMNATURALLY.CO.UK

Naturally Healthy Dogs

Raw Food Deliveries across

East Anglia

07590 621636

www.NaturallyHealthyDogs.co.uk

Fireworks! 5 Tips For Keeping Fearful Pets Calm

Ihor Basko, DVM, CVA
Kauai, Hawaii

Here's a question that keeps coming up: *"What can I do to help my fearful pet cope with fireworks?"*

I've found that the fireworks stress many livestock (especially horses) and pets (mainly dogs) over the weekend. Pets with heart problems, or those who are ill and weak, are most susceptible.

So here's some helpful tips to keep your pets calm in the middle of a fire-storm!

1. Keep them confined in a safe place:

Dogs and cats have a tendency to get spooked by the loud noises and will take off running through the neighborhood. This puts them at risk of getting lost and/or getting hit a by car, so it's best to keep your pets confined in a small, dark, cozy area (like a bathroom, or in a small bedroom…somewhere indoors is ideal). I don't recommend keeping dogs chained outdoors or keeping pets confined in a garage (too many fumes present from common chemicals stored in the garage).

Avoid taking your pets outdoors (beaches, parks, etc.) during the peak hours of fireworks celebrations (usually around dusk til midnight or so).

And keep your horses/livestock confined in a barn too — you don't want them spooking in an open pasture with barbed wire fencing!

2. Create a calm, cave-like environment.

You'll want to create a cave-like atmosphere for your pets to feel most secure during this time. Close the windows, close the curtains, and turn on the central air or fans, and place your pet's kennel (door kept open) in a corner of the room (covered by a blanket or towel) and allow your pet the option to go into or come out of the kennel. Whatever he/she is comfortable with. I've found that cats seem to feel most comfortable in the bathroom with a litter box, water, music, and toys…and lots of places to hide.

Playing soft music or turning on the TV (any kind of mellow ambient noise) will also help distract your pets from the loud bangs and pops of the fireworks. Classical music is great (like Bach or Mozart), or you could try playing animal (whale and dolphin sounds for dogs, bird sounds for cats) or nature (ocean, rivers, rain) sounds. Horses seem to enjoy country music — no joke! :)

3. Make sure your pets are wearing ID tags.

In case your pet gets lost in the commotion of the holiday, make sure he or she is wearing a collar with an ID tag. The tag should include your pet's name and your number, and possibly your address. This is a good practice even if your pet already has an internal microchip.

4. Exercise your dogs and tire them out.

Here's a tip from Honolulu animal behaviourist, Wendy Mah: *"Exercise and keep dogs active during the day. Don't let them laze around too much (but keep them out of the sun) and encourage them to walk, play, run, hike, etc. Tire them out! Ball and game playing using treat rewards work well. Then, when night arrives, they'll be sleeping or be too tired to get too worked up about the fireworks."*

5. Try out Calming Agents.

It's best to try these out ahead of time so you can see how it affects your pet.

Drugs: Check with your veterinarian for recommendations. These may depress breathing and lower blood pressure. And pets should not be geriatric, have heart disease, high blood pressure (cats), or be on other medications. Valium in general is safer than Acepromazine which could cause a "freak out" reaction and/or reduce blood pressure too much!

Thundershirt: This is a cloth wrap that will put light pressure on your pet. This compression is thought to be calming. It was originally designed for pets that were fearful of thunderstorms but it could be equally effective for calming pets during fireworks displays. You can find these at most pet stores and some veterinary clinics.

Muscle relaxers:

- Magnesium (ascorbate, glycinate, citrate): Give 100 to 500mg orally, twice daily (may cause loose stools)
- Bath soak: You can also try soaking your pet in a mix of epsom salts and valerian and chamo-

mile teas. Use warm water.

Serotonin enhancers:

- 5 HTP (L-typtophan): Give 25 to 100mg twice a day

- L-theanine: Give 100 to 500mg, twice daily

Nervines (calms nerves):

- B-complex B1,3,6

- Valerian (should not be taken with Valium)

- Chamomile

- Passion Flower

- Calms Forte Homeopathic (very safe)

- Oyster Shell: Give 1,000 to 3,000mg twice daily

- Dragon Bone

- Vitamin B complex

- Quiet Moments by NaturVet (chamomile, passion fruit, tryptophan and Bcomplex)

- Stress Away by VetClassics (chamomile, passion fruit, tryptophan and melatonin

- Anxiety and Stress Support by RESOURCES (B complex, melatonin, passion flower, chamomile, oyster shell, ginkgo, zizziphus, schizandra, melatonin, cat's claw, and Chinese herbs). Especially good to use with dogs with heart problems or dementia.

Sleep inducers:

- Melatonin: Give ½ to 6 milligrams every 8 hours

Emotional / Disturbed Shen/ Heart Weakness:

- Bach Flower Remedies

These are just a few suggestions. Ask your local holistic vet for specific recommendations/dosages for your pet.

www.drbasko.com

radio show: Pets People and Paradise...... Saturdays from 11 am to noon Pacific time.

listen online at: www.kkcr.org

DR. IHOR BASKO, DVM

In June Healthful Dog hosted our first

Holistic Pet Health Conference

and it was an outstanding success.

We were honoured to show a weeks worth of lectures from leading professional holistic animal health practitioners around the Globe.
Including:

- Dr. Ian Billinghurst
- Dr. Christina Chambreau
- Dr. Peter Dobias
- Dr. Jodie Gruenstern
- Dr. Wendy Jensen
- Dr. Patricia Jordan
- Susan Thixton

and experts in:

- Acupressure
- Animal Communication
- Feldenkrais
- Flower Essences
- Sound Therapy
- Bowen
- Behaviour

If you missed it we are now able to bring you unlimited access via our new Training Centre.

Get full unlimited access for only

£47

https://healthfuldog.zenler.com/course

And you can now pre-register to attend next years conference:

http://eepurl.com/cTllbf

http://www.HolisticPetHealthConference.co.uk

Image Source: www.copperclothing.co.uk

Discover the Antimicrobial Power of Copper for Protecting Dogs against Yeast and Skin Infections

Kunal Patel

Dogs are prone to skin allergies and yeast infections, particularly when they get older or fall sick. If the health of their skin is compromised, it's easier for yeast and bacteria to grow on it, causing itchiness and bad odours. When your pet scratches these itchy spots, they get hot, inflamed or swollen due to increased blood flow, making the problem even worse.

Skin problems are particularly common among many popular breeds, and knowing about these can help you prevent or manage them before they become serious.

Which Breeds Are at Risk of Skin and Yeast Infections?

While any dog may have skin problems or yeast infections, these 10 breeds are generally at higher risk:

Spaniels – Their long, floppy ears and heavy jowls put spaniels at risk of numerous skin problems. They are especially prone to infections in the folds of their lower lip and their ears, which provide the ideal environment for the growth of bacteria and yeast.

Cocker Spaniels – Cocker Spaniels are prone to eye problems and ear infections as well as a higher risk of seborrhea. This genetic condition leads to the chronic growth of a waxy substance on the ears, and may also cause greasy, scaly or smelly skin.

Boxers – These compact, muscular and athletic dogs often face a wide range of serious health concerns, including cancer, hip dysplasia, arthritis, knee and heart-related problems, thyroid issues etc. They're also susceptible to skin allergies and infections.

Standard Poodles – Poodles are prone to developing granulomatous sebaceous adenitis, an inherited skin condition that affects the oil glands. In addition to making them more prone to secondary skin infections, this condition can also cause hair loss.

Chinese Shar-Peis – With short-haired dogs like Shar-Peis and bulldogs, skin irritation is a common problem. Folds in their skin cause short hairs on one side to poke against the other side when the dog moves, causing irritation and making allergies or skin infections worse. Young English bulldogs are also prone to skin tumours called histiocytomas.

American Bulldogs – Along with irritation caused by skin folds and short hair, this breed tends to have food and environmental allergies that affect the health of their skin. They may also inherit canine ichthyosiform dermatoses, a condition that causes skin along the armpits, groin and belly to become red and scaly.

Basset Hounds – Large sad eyes and droopy ears make these dogs look adorable, and they love sniffing everything they can reach. Coupled with their short legs and droopy skin, this raises the risk of picking up infection-causing bacteria, viruses and parasites, or even inhaling them.

Doberman Pinschers – These dogs often have low thyroid function or hyperthyroidism, which affects their skin health. Hyperthyroidism can lead to alopecia or hair loss, especially along the flanks, while low thyroid function may cause a dry or flaky coat. Both issues can lead to secondary skin infections as well.

Labrador Retrievers – Labradors are generally robust and healthy as long as they get a good diet and plenty of exercise. However, they can face allergies due to dietary, genetic and environmental factors, causing skin problems such as itchiness, hot spots, etc.

Pit Bull Terriers – A weak immune system makes pit bulls more prone to infections, as well as issues caused by tiny demodex mites that reside in hair follicles. In dogs with low immunity, demodectic outbreaks can cause secondary skin infections or itchiness.

In addition to the breeds listed above, dogs with hormonal imbalances, excessive earwax, weak immunity and food, environmental or genetic allergies also face a higher risk of skin and yeast infections. Certain medications such as antibiotics, or warm and humid living environments can also pose a threat.

How Does Copper Help with Treating Skin Problems?

Copper is not only an essential mineral found in all mammals, but its additional health benefits for your canine companion include:

• Incredible antimicrobial powers, which kill a huge variety of bacteria, fungi and viruses through contact. Historically, copper has also been used to fight fleas, mites and other parasites that affect household pets.

• Eliminating bad odours from your pet's fur, skin and bedding. These unwanted odours are usually caused by sweat, bacteria and fungi, and copper effectively fights this nasty mixture in a safe and chemical-free manner.

Boosting blood flow, circulation and regulation of body temperature. Copper helps keep your dog warm and comfortable, and can even provide relief from arthritis, joint pain and other mobility issues in older canines.

Owning a dog is a huge responsibility, since they need as much love, care and attention as a young child. Copper beds and blankets are a great way to help your furry friends stay healthier and happier, so switch to them today!

Author Bio:

Kunal is a young and passionate entrepreneur, fascinated by the workings of the human body and natural solutions for common health problems. He's single-minded in his aim to make Copper Defence a brand that's recognised across the globe, by partnering with global brands to make these high-tech materials easily accessible for everyone. If you'd like to get in touch, email Kunal at kunal@copperdefence.com or visit copperclothing.co.uk for copper-infused clothing, pet accessories and more.

Pet Loss Oasis

Nurturing the heart and soul of people grieving animals

Vetting Your Vet

Making sure your vet is a partner, not a protagonist, in your animal's end of life care

By **Sue Reid**

Intuitive Animal communicator, Energy Healer and Animal End-of-Life Supporter

Throughout your animal's life, vets may or may not have figured prominently. For most animals at some point, a vet is needed even if just for routine health care (no, not annual vaccinations and routine chemical wormers, see elsewhere in this magazine!). If you follow a holistic approach you may well have given considerable thought to your choice of vet, which can only stand you in good stead as your animal gets older. But if you've just used a local vet as and when necessary, suddenly finding that your animal has a life limiting diagnosis can raise questions you may not have thought of before.

For me personally, there was no doubt that having a holistic vet who knew my Tilly-Terrier inside out, who had all sorts of alternatives to the chemical meds which Til often couldn't tolerate, who was very straight with us but with whom we could discuss absolutely any aspect of Tilly's care including her own end-of-life wishes, was the rock on which her whole journey stood. It was what made the magic possible. We valued this so much we even moved house to be near the Practice.

But not everyone has these choices available, and there is no doubt that there is a serious shortage of holistic or integrated veterinary practices. So what do you do if you're suddenly faced with a change in your animal's veterinary needs?

The following seven questions aim to help you decide whether you can remain with your current prac-tice, or whether a change may be in order.

Do you trust your vet/practice?

No matter whether you're looking for a holistic or allopathic approach, this question should be at the heart of your decision. Your precious animal's life is in their hands, literally. I hear too many stories from heartbroken people who felt they were pressurised to make a euthanasia decision before they truly felt it was time. I also have a friend who is a dog groomer, who quotes stories from some of her human customers to the effect that they feel they're having to be on guard every minute against their vet recommending (often expensive) tests and procedures that cover the vet in case of any legal claim but don't actually change the treatment protocol for the animal.

I am fully aware of the hornet's nest these issues potentially are, and they are not for discussion here. There are always two sides to any story. I really believe all vets wish to do their best for the animals in their care. But I also believe some are limited in their views, especially around an animal's emotional needs as well as physical. I also believe that in hopefully few instances, bringing income to the practice (justified by "being thorough" and/or avoiding potential lawsuits), takes the place of common sense, especially with very elderly or poorly animals.

So consider your experiences with your current vet/

practice. Are you confident that you and they can be their partners in supporting and protecting your animal at own this very precious time? views

and

rea-

Does your vet agree with your aims for your animal?

You may want to seek any cure possible, no matter sons, of what the cost, including possible short term stress course, for your animal such as chemotherapy or surgery; or which you may have decided that palliative care (treating you or managing symptoms rather than seeking a cure) would to give the best quality of life for the longest time. listen to Or a combination of the two may be possible, de- before pending upon circumstances...... What if your vet decid-disagrees with your aims?

Do you use intuitive communication with your ani-ing), is this going to create an undercurrent of ten-mal? Do you believe you know what he or she sion, or even potentially a battle ground, at a time wants, in relation to treatment or quality of life in when harmony and positivity is vital? general? And if you do, does your vet at least ac-commodate and work with you around this?

Whatever you decide, you are your animal's guardi-an. You know him/her better than anyone else. Ob-viously you will rely greatly on the advice of your

Does your vet offer house calls? And if not, is the journey to the surgery "do-able" with a potential-ly very poorly animal?

trusted vet, who should have the medical You may need or prefer a home visit, for treatment knowledge and practical experience you need at to spare your animal the stress of travel and the this time. But you both have to be able to work to-"vet surgery" experience. And you certainly may pre-gether in your animal's best interests. If your goals fer euthanasia to be carried out at home if that be-are different this could be a challenge, and you comes necessary. Not all vets offer this option, so need to ask why you're not in agreement. Does your it's worth asking beforehand. And if they do, what vet feel you're unrealistic in your hopes? Maybe are their charges? they're right, maybe not. Seek a second opinion, unless your animal is in uncontrollable pain or his/ If they don't, think carefully about under what cir-her suffering cannot be managed. cumstances surgery visits may be needed, and how that might work. Maybe not too bad if you, or a will-ing helper, drives. But if you're using public transport, this question may be a deal breaker.

Do you want to follow a holistic, minimum chemical route where possible?

What out-of-hours cover is on offer? Are you happy that it will meet your animal's need and yours?

And if so, does your vet offer that, or would they be happy for you to refer out to other vets or therapists Even with our own wonderful vet, we would have as necessary? preferred a fully integrated out of hours cover ser-vice, as we had a few overnight challenges. But it This comes back to being able to work together. If just wasn't practical and with everything else so your vet, however lovely, is completely against any good, it was a compromise we gladly settled for. approach you want to try (and they are entitled to

Regarding home euthanasia, there are some vet practices who have set up recently in the UK who specialise in 24/7 end of life support and home euthanasia services, see the Resources list at the end of this article. This may be a compromise if you want to keep your current vet but would really prefer that your animal was able to die in his or her own familiar home with all the family, including other animals, around if they wanted to be.

What are their views on managing the end of life?

Would they support you though a pain-free natural passing for your dog if that's what you'd prefer if it's possible (depending on diagnosis, it may not be.) Will they agree with you about the right time for euthanasia if that's your choice? Will they take the time to discuss the options and really listen to your views and concerns? Or is there a risk that you will feel over-ruled or dismissed?

Are they the person you would want to be there to help your dog when/if the time comes for euthanasia?

Emergencies happen, and sometimes there is no time for choices, in the cause of the animal's welfare. But most of the animal people I know have preferences for who they would want to be there when it's time to say goodbye. A vet who will give them time, answer any questions, be empathic and comfortable with the process so they can feel confident that their beloved animal is in the best possible hands at this precious time, and that their preferences will be honoured. Because there will never be a second chance to get it right....

If you've answered NO to any of the above questions, think seriously about changing your vet at this point. You may have to travel further, which obviously has implications regarding treatment and emergencies. But having to struggle at every turn to achieve the care you want for your animal adds huge stress at an already overwhelming time.

To find the closest holistic vet to you, visit the British Association of Homeopathic Veterinary Surgeons, see Resources for link.

If changing is simply not possible, prepare to be assertive. Your vet is the medical expert. But you know your animal better than anyone else. And you're a paying customer. You may come through this experience tougher, and with more negotiation and people-management skills than you ever knew you had. And that may be one of your animal's gifts to you....

Holly's Homecoming

We had a very recent experience of the need for assertiveness, about our friend's little Shih Tzu, Holly. Holly is 18 years old. She has a heart murmur to match Niagara, and her sight and hearing are not good. She looks what she is, an old lady. But she's a little toughie through and through – she has never suffered fools gladly and has only rarely understood the word "No" when applied to herself. A total star.....

Holly began to wheeze quite badly one weekend when her usual, much loved and trusted vet was unavailable. We took her and her human Mum to the 24 hour emergency vet, some distance away. She was improving all the way in the car – she lay on my knee and although I could feel her chest "crackling" at first, it settled well. She'd stopped wheezing by the time we got into the surgery.

The vet we saw was young, practical and thorough. Nothing wrong with that. We explained that Holly's usual vet was unavailable but if she could be made more comfortable we would take her to her own vet tomorrow. He listened to Holly's chest, said "That's a bit crackly", told us that any treatment may or may not work and we should be prepared for the worst. We said we were, but she had already improved this morning and we wanted to try. Then he said he needed full bloods before any medication could be given and results would be back this afternoon. He took Holly's collar off and lifted her up. Her human Mum was speechless with horror. We said "Do you mean you're going to admit her??" He looked surprised at our surprise, and said "Yes." We said "Is this essential? She's already improving, we can hear that – she can see her own vet tomorrow – and she's 18, she can barely see or hear, she'll be so scared and upset to be away from her home and her family. Could she not just have some short term help to be more comfortable?"

He looked doubtful, but we, including her Mum who had regained her voice, were adamant. So Holly had a diuretic injection which she accepted with unusual good grace, and some tablets to support her until she was able to see her own vet. We agreed we would bring her straight back if she deteriorated again, which we would certainly have done. And home she went, not wheezing. Her condition maintained; she saw her own vet, who put her on new medication and said we had done exactly the right thing in bringing her home. She was bright, eating again, and she was still Holly.

We could have got it wrong, and Holly may have died through not staying in. Realistically, she could die at any time. We all knew this too. But Holly's Mum said that if we had given in, and Holly had died away from home, scared and lonely, she would never have forgiven herself. It was all about comfort and freedom from fear. It was a judgement call, and it paid off on this occasion. And there was no doubt in our minds about what Holly wanted.....

So – the moral of this article, and this story, is first consider what you **need** from your vet; know what you ideally want; and consider what compromises you're prepared to make, for your animal's sake and your family's. Be open-minded, but prepare to be assertive if you have to. Remember that when this journey is over, you want to be able to look back with as few regrets as possible. The better your relationship with your vet, the easier and smoother this already hugely challenging time will

be – for you, and for your much-loved animal. And that's what it's all about.....

Until next time, much love to you all, of every species,

Sue

Resources

British Association of Homeopathic Veterinary Surgeons - www.bahvs.com

Home euthanasia directory UK - www.dignified-departures.co.uk

Sue Reid and Elaine Downs

Partners, *Animal Matters*

Email: animalmatters@aol.com

Website: www.animalcommunication.co.uk

Animal Matters *in the Media*

What Does Biologically Appropriate Mean?

Kimberly Morris Gauthier

SuperZoo 2017 in Las Vegas, Nevada, was the biggest SuperZoo in the history of the event. SuperZoo is an annual trade show where pet brands have an opportunity to display new and existing products, network with retailers and industry guests, and speak with the press.

This was my third year attending and I tracked 17,000 steps per day walking the showroom floor and on the second day, I saw something that made me stop in my tracks. A presentation by a popular Canadian dry dog food brand that has trademarked the words "biologically appropriate."

During the show, there was a presentation where they showed the food that goes into making their kibble. I was impressed by the massive amount of food waste that occurred on the stage and the repetition of "biologically appropriate" and "prey model." And as I walked the showroom floor, I saw that many dry dog food brands were co-opting terms found in raw feeding.

- Biologically appropriate

- Species appropriate

- Ancestral diet

- Prey model

- Raw food diet

Those of us in the raw feeding and natural rearing community understand that there is nothing raw or natural about a diet of dry dog food, however, the average pet owner may not understand the difference. Flashy commercials and big marketing budgets are doing a great job of spin.

In an attempt to correct the narrative, I decided to start from the beginning and ask, "is kibble biologically appropriate?"

What Does Biologically Appropriate Mean?

Biologically appropriate is food that is appropriate for a dog's digestive system. Dogs are carnivores and in nature, the best food would be live, fresh food - smaller animals (whole prey) - that provide the living enzymes, antioxidants, and other nutrients needed for our dogs to thrive.

Biologically appropriate has been used correctly to market raw dog food. Dry dog food companies are using the term in an effort to convince pet lovers that kibble is closer to what a dog's ancestor, the grey wolf, would have consumed.

I'm shaking my head too.

5 Reasons Why Kibble isn't Biologically Appropriate

During the presentation, the brand added whole raw meat to a container to show us how much "real" meat and "fresh" ingredients they used. What they didn't address was the process that turns whole raw meat into small, hard nuggets.

1. Kibble isn't biologically appropriate because it's cooked multiple times. The hard food that is created is difficult to digest, contains no moisture, and puts our dogs in a constant state of dehydration.

2. Kibble isn't biologically appropriate because it's filled with synthetic nutrients to replace the nutrients lost during the processing. While synthetic vitamins may help the food meet AAFCO standard, it's difficult for dogs to absorb these nutrients.

3. Kibble contains carbs or grain, which increase the risk of exposure to moulds and storage mites, which lead to allergies in many dogs.

4. Kibble doesn't clean teeth. The ripping and tearing into raw meat and bones provide this benefit.

5. Kibble doesn't contain living enzymes needed to promote a healthy digestive system and any probiotics added to kibble are long dead and useless before a consumer gets the bag home.

The pet food industry is trying to convince pet owners that dry dog food is what dogs were meant to eat, however, dry dog food is less than 100 years old. Dogs have been around for significantly longer. While dogs have adapted to a diet of kibble, it's not biologically appropriate for the canine species.

http://keepthetailwagging.com/

KEEP THE TAIL

EST.   2011

WAGGING®

MY DOGS EAT BETTER THAN I DO

Lungworm Awareness

Caroline Hearn

Lungworm is a parasitic nematode which is increasingly becoming a threat to dogs all across the UK. What started as a few isolated cases has now spread, so most counties have seen dogs infected with it to some degree.

This could be due to a milder and wetter climate providing a perfect environment for slugs and snails to thrive and a large increase in the urban fox population. Dogs that freely wander in fields and near streams are also more likely to pick up the parasite.

There are three main types of lungworm that dogs are most likely to become infected with:

Oslerus osleri (dog lungworm) **Crenosoma Vulpis** (fox lungworm) **and Angiostrongylus vasosum**

After having one of my own dogs contract fox lungworm earlier this year it is a particularly nasty parasite that is often overlooked or misdiagnosed so it is important to be aware and vigilant of any symptoms that your dog may develop and know what the options for treatment and prevention are.

Life cycle

The lungworm needs a host such as a slug, snail or fox in which to grow and develop. The dog, sometimes accidentally eats a slug possibly on a blade of grass, stuck to a dog toy, in a water bowl or comes into contact with infected fox faeces, often by rolling in it. Dogs that eat the dropping of other animals such as horses, sheep & deer can consume slugs without even being aware that they are there.

Three days after ingestion the larvae can be found in the dogs stomach where they then proceed to migrate through the body until reaching the lungs. The larvae mature and start laying eggs which are coughed up by the dog , enter the stomach and are expelled within the faeces. Slugs and snails are partial to dog poop so they become infected with the larvae to start to cycle again.

The life cycle of the Crenosoma fox lungworm is similar except the adult worms live in the airways of the lungs and the trachea.

The parasite doesn`t pass directly from dog to dog and my other two dogs have exactly the same lifestyle yet were unaffected. The larvae do however pass out in the faeces of the infected dog so there is the potential for the infection to be spread that way.

Symptoms

The biggest worry with lungworm is that sometimes there are no symptoms present until the disease is at a critical level. This is why regular testing is so important.

The most common symptoms present are:

- General lethargy and intolerance to exercise

- Breathing difficulties and noisy inhalation

- Loss of weight and condition

- Sore throat, developing a cough or gag reflex and air licking

- Unsettled, starring into space and a change of character

- Discharge or bleeding from the nostrils

- Chest infection, bronchitis or pneumonia

- Pale mucus membranes of the eyes and gums

- Profuse bleeding even from a tiny wound

- Collapse and seizures

Fox lungworm is rarely fatal to dogs unless there are secondary complications such as chest infections, pneumonia etc. Angiostrongylus on the other hand can often be fatal if left untreated due to the increased risk of haemorrhage and seizures.

Diagnosis

There are a number of ways to test if your dog is carrying lungworm. The method I used to confirm that my dog was infected was a faecal worm count. This involves collecting a small sample of your dogs faeces for 3 consecutive days then sending off in a secure pot either to a veterinary surgery or a company that specialises in this service. They will then look for larvae in the stool sample. The results are back within a couple of days and will give a negative or positive result and state the level of infestation.

The downside of this particular test is that due to the intermittent shedding of larvae by this particular parasite it is possible to get a negative result even though the dog has lungworm, as shedding of larvae may not be taking place over the days the sample was taken. Regular testing every 3 months is recommended for lungworm or earlier should you see any symptoms of the dog being infected.

A relatively new blood test is now available in some surgeries called the Angio detect test. This detects a specific antigen in the blood when Angiostrongylus vasosum is present. The results are back in clinic within 15 minutes.

The Baermann test can be used where the stool sample is suspended in water causing the larvae to merge with the water then to sink to the bottom of the vessel ready for collection.

A tracheal flush or chest x-rays can also be used for diagnosis

Treatment

Due to the seriousness and secondary complications that can develop from carrying any of the lungworm parasites it is advised to treat the dog with an anthelmintic specifically targeted to killing lungworm.

This was a real dilemma for me as I haven`t given chemical wormers to my dogs in many years, preferring instead to use a worm count which had until that point always returned a "no worms found" result.

As my dogs health and breathing started to deteriorate and a second chest infection started to take hold it was a necessary thing to do. I chose to go with a seven day course of Panacur and as long as he was showing improvement then the plan was to test initially every two months then every three months thereafter. At the same time I started the Verm-x liquid.

There are a number of products which either kill or reduce the numbers of lungworm, so thoroughly research what is best for your dog. The drug group Ivermectin is contraindicated in Collies who can be particularly sensitive to it.

My dog, even with a low infestation became very ill, developed chest & throat infections had difficulty breathing and a very sore throat. He still makes a slight noise on inhalation which I can only assume is damage from the lungworm and in time will hopefully improve.

He was given pre and probiotics to support his gut, as not only did he have a large amount of chemical wormer but also two courses of antibiotics .

A mixture of slippery elm, marshmallow, liquorice, ginger, thyme and a little fresh garlic were offered in either natural goats yogurt or bone broth as his throat was so sore he found eating difficult and painful. Feeding from a raised bowl also helped him become more comfortable.

Prevention

It is thought that once a dog has had lungworm it does develop a certain degree of immunity as long as the threat is not too great and certain precautions are taken to prevent reinfection.

Fox lungworm is on our land where the dogs are exercised so we have to be particularly vigilant.

Verm-X This is my chosen method of prevention at present. It comes in biscuit or liquid form and is a completely natural product which creates an environment that worms particularly dislike. As lungworm are present in the gut for a short period of time before migrating elsewhere in the body there is only a small window of opportunity to influence the parasites with any natural methods. Therefore it is recommended at a higher rate to target lungworm and given for longer periods of time.

So far we are sending stool samples off every 3 months and each result has returned as negative to lungworm.

Slugs & Snails are attracted to dog poo so it is crucial that any faeces are picked up as soon as possible before contamination occurs. It is also really important to bring in any feed and water bowls and dog toys so that slugs and snails don't have access to them over night. Also not encouraging foxes into the garden by feeding them will lessen the risk.

Use humane traps for slugs and snails if there are a large number of them in the garden.

If your dog eats copious amounts of grass then adding green leafy veg & herbs to their diet can reduce the urge to eat so much of it as they may be craving the chlorophyll or fibre it contains.

I also feed my own herbal blend that contains neem leaf which is an age old parasite preventative and echinacea to help give the immune system a boost.

Caroline Hearn MICHT Dip ICAT

www.Hedgerow-Hounds.co.uk

Mugly's 'Doggy Dementia' charity collar
by Tallulah Couture

Mugly has C.C.D. aka 'Doggy dementia' and as part of his bucket list, he wants to raise £2500 for Cinque ports rescue. He asked his friends at Tallulah Couture and they were happy to help

This Tallulah Couture exclusive design comes in four sizes. £6 from each collar sale will be donated to Cinque Ports rescue.

check out facebook.com/uglymugly or bev@uglymugly.co.uk

Nonverbal Communication with Our Dogs and Cats

Celeste Yarnall, Ph.D

Nonverbal communication is a gift that all living beings share, one you'll need to reawaken to better interact with and care for your animal companions. Most dog and cat lovers already understand canine and feline body language, which is one non-verbal technique. But you can use your other, natural, nonverbal communication skills, and actually begin to see things through your dog or cat's eyes, and become his/her voice.

You can learn animal communication by taking a class or reading some of the great books available today on the subject. But many of the basics are so simple that we can easily begin nonverbally communicating right away. Remember, long before humans had spoken language, we were able to communicate among ourselves and with the animals; it is a kind of heart to heart communication skill that we all possess.

Did you ever know a set of twins who said they each knew what the other was thinking, or you heard your mother say she had "woman's intuition" or "just knew something was wrong." Have you ever had an image of a friend come to mind and then received a phone call from that very person saying,"I was just thinking about you and wanted to say hello"? These are all examples of nonverbal communication.

Those of us fortunate enough to have been raised with animal companions probably "talked" to them all the time—and they "talked" back—without words. You didn't have to be Dr. Doolittle to do it, either. You may have chalked up your own memories of such experiences to an overly active imagination. But it's far more likely that, as a child, you were still unencumbered by belief systems that would tell you otherwise.

You can try it anytime with your own dog or cat, simply by listening to your heart, instead of to your head with its endless, meaningless chatter. Just let those thoughts pass by you, and relax and breathe deeply. You're going to visualize your furry companion coming over to you. Close your eyes so that you focus on every detail: the feeling of your dog or cats lovely coat, those deep, trusting eyes staring up at you, and imagine him walking toward you. Often, even the first time you try it, your cat or dog will be by your side before you know it, so happy that you've communicated with him at long last, in his own way.

Please don't worry about whether you're "doing it right." Not every person (or animal) is visually oriented. Visualization is just like imagining or remembering. It may come as actual pictures, like a movie, or as sounds, or a voice, or as feelings, or just a sense of "knowing." Any way you receive the information is valid.

It is very important to always communicate in positive terms— "see" what you want your dog or cat to do, rather than focusing on unwanted behaviours. Dogs and cats live fully in the moment, so picture them as you want them to be. For instance, don't ask them if they want to go to the vet or the groomer or for a ride in the car. Why? Because, they don't know how they'll feel until they get there to that exact moment in time. Unlike us, dogs and cats live in the moment. What lessons we can learn about being here—right now! So visualize them peacefully riding in the car, or calmly allowing the vet to examine them.

Practice visualizing positive, loving pictures rather than negative, worrying ones. Have you noticed that the things you worry about often seem to happen? Practice positivity, and positive visualization, and you'll find it spilling over into every aspect of your life.

This is so crucial when communicating with your animal companions. If you say, for example (either out loud or nonverbally), "Don't jump on the couch," your dog or cat sees an image in your mind's eye of him jumping on the couch. He won't get the "don't" part of it. He'll think oh, she wants me to jump on the couch. Your yelling at him to not jump on the couch is then a mixed signal. Instead, say and visualize what you DO want him to do. In this case, you would say, in an even but stern tone, "Go to your bed!" Then gently carry or lead him to his bed to reinforce the positive behaviour.

It's impossible to hide your feelings from dogs and cats. They always know—and they may "get it" even before we know ourselves. They can even take on your stresses, fears, and frustrations. Over time, these may manifest as illness. So it's a good idea to even refrain from arguing in front of your animal companions; it's extremely stressful for them. It's not fair to treat them as if they're not in the room when we lose control of our emotions. Their sensibilities should be respected.

To give you an idea how sensitive dogs are, Rupert

Sheldrake, a British biologist and the author of Dogs That Know When Their Owners are Coming Home, did an experiment in which he placed video cameras with time codes in the house, aimed to catch the action of the homebound dog. At a random time, unbeknownst to the human or dog, the human would get a phone call on a cell phone many miles away, saying to return home. At that very instant, cameras showed that the homebound dog would become excited and run to the door to wait for their human. This experiment was repeated hundreds of times, and were all confirmed by the videos. The moral of this story: don't feel silly practicing nonverbal communication, EVER!

Most Interesting Article 2016

You can also practice this pure heart-to-heart communication skill with a new pet, or with animals at dog or cat shows or shelters, or even at your vets office. First, learn the cat or dog's name, if possible. Try saying the name in a sweet, soft, "feminine" (high-pitched) voice. We pretty much all do that with animals and babies, right? It seems, in the animal world the female voice is the most non-threatening. If you're a man, or a woman with a deep voice, raise your pitch and speak softly. Of course, always ask the guardian if it's okay to work with and touch the animal; and then ask the animal's permission.

To start, if you can, get down a bit lower than normal (ideally, at the animal's eye level) and imagine the dog or cat sitting on the floor of your own home. You may get a response as a picture of what his own home looks like from his point of view. Perhaps you can distinguish the outlines of a bed or the legs of a coffee table from underneath: what the dog sees from that perspective. Your image may look like a black-and-white negative, reverse image, rather than

a normal photo type memory.

If you don't get a picture, it doesn't mean you're not doing it right. The dog may just be telling you he's not allowed in that room. Trust yourself and the feelings that come up and continue to listen with your heart. Accept the images or feelings you do get, and go on. He may tell you something about what he likes or dislikes. Or he may be content exactly where he is right now. Keep going anyway, and just let him talk through his own senses.

What are you getting? Is he showing you what his floors look or feel like? Do cold, slippery floors make him nervous because he skids on them? Now visualize the cat or dog's feeding area. What kind of food does he eat? Do you taste or feel any textures in your mouth? What about water? Is it fresh and clean? What has he smelled recently? He may change the picture you send to reflect his truth, and he may present it to all of your senses or just some of them.

As you continue, do you see other animals where he lives? Send him a picture of one of your animal companions. What does he say to that? What does he like to play with? Cats may have little balls and catnip toys, and dogs may have chew toys, tennis balls, or maybe even a Frisbee. Give him these images and see what you get back. If his human companion is there, ask questions to help you assess your images. After you present an image to him, remember to leave a space for him to answer.

As you read the impressions your animal friend is sending. You may receive feelings of space and expansion if he has room to play and places to rest in—or feelings of contraction if he's been caged or otherwise too restricted.

Perhaps you may feel he's trying to tell you about an aggressive person. This person may not necessarily be a man; it could be a woman or child with a strong personality—dogs and cats sense human beings as personalities, not as men and women. Ask the dog or cat non verbally how he likes this person. He may wish the person would leave him alone, or he may enjoy playing with the person but can't understand why he gets scolded for playing too roughly.

You can use your nonverbal skills to assess the animal's well-being through a mental body scan. Just look at the animal, starting with the head and working down the back to the tip of the tail. How do you feel compared with how you felt before scanning? If you feel anything unusual as you continue your scan, you may be on to something. Ask the dog or cat, using his name, how he feels as you move along his body with your eyes.

If you don't have permission to touch the animal, you can pet the cat or dog's aura. This is more subtle, but just as effective. Think how you'd feel if a perfect stranger just started stroking you without your consent. Then when you use this indirect way of laying on hands by petting the space around the body (which is referred to as the etheric double), you can often feel the animal's energy and determine whether he is receptive to your touch, which after all will leave your scent on this dog or cat. By using the etheric double area you will find that this in itself is a valuable avenue of communication and diagnosis, and through it you can offer much healing, especially when you use love as the catalyst.

As you practice, your skills will improve. When doing a mental body scan, you may feel discomfort in certain parts of your own body. While this is important information, you do not need to hold it in your body. Simply release the feeling and say to yourself, "This animal's feelings are his own. I release them." In your mind's eye, wrap the dog or cat in healing white light, or say a prayer or blessing. Then "turn off" the discomfort, much as you would the TV when it transmits images you don't like. As simply as you would change the channel; just change the subject. It is never necessary to be the recipient of any other being's pain.

Nonverbal communication seems to come most easily with other people's animals. It's sometimes difficult to practice with our own furry friends because we are so emotionally involved with them. Gradually you'll develop a proficiency that you can then apply at home. Most folks do their best communicating with their own animal companions through play. Through play we express and hear verbal, non-verbal, body language, and other communications.

Be sure to talk to your animal companions about their day. Sometimes if you have more than one then they compete to communicate with us all at once. Just give them the time and the space to get it all off their chests. Remember, they knew you were coming home long before you got there as Sheldrake proved, and have been happily waiting to talk to you!

Nonverbal communication can greatly expand your relationship with animals, but some dogs and cats are reserved, just like certain people are. They simply don't want to converse. Don't be discouraged. And some people never get pictures, only feelings; and that's fine. Trust yourself, and proceed with openness, imagination and confidence. You're on your way to being a nonverbal communications expert and experience for yourself that the intelligence and spirit in all life!

———————————————

N.B. Celeste was suddenly diagnosed with Cancer at the end of 2014 and yet has not missed a beat when it comes to ensuring that our magazine has copy, even sending it from hospital in the middle of chemotherapy or post-op, please help her to cover the uninsured costs she and her husband need to find in order to get healthy again with as much natural treatment as possible via her gofundme page:

http://www.gofundme.com/kvo9xs

Thank You

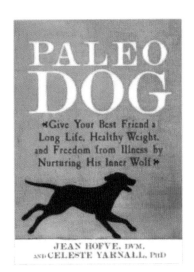

What kind of "doctor" are you?

Dr. Patricia Jordan

I have a double doctorate, one in veterinary medicine like every other vet that is licensed and dully certified. The other is my more worthy doctorate, in naturopathic medicine. One doctorate training program taught me the fundamentals on "how" the body worked; anatomy, physiology, and the other taught me how to identify disease at the root and to use natural medicines and therapies to allow the body to heal itself. Veterinary medicine did not teach me about the immune system nor did it teach me the science of nutrition as the root. As a result it was the second doctorate program, the one in naturopathic medicine that is so vital to my work as a healer.

After my veterinary medical degree, I was invited to enter a PhD program in Georgia in Veterinary Microbiology. I would be able to follow my Honors Research in Medical Microbiology. If I had accepted the position, I would probably be at the CDC in Atlanta or Emory Medical College still working in Microbiology. Instead, I worked for a decade in general practice, quickly realizing I hadn't enough training to handle what I was seeing in the trenches, on the front line of general practice. I started to "stray outside the lines" as they call it. I went to find a better way to serve my patients.

Besides the doctorate in naturopathic medicine, completing professional programs for dully certified veterinarians in Homeopathy, both the Basic and the Professional Course under Dr. Richard Pitcairn was completed. I completed a year of volunteer work answering questions from the public about homeopathy for animals. Most of the questions coming into free service were about animals that became dis eased following vaccinations and those questions were directed to me for the answers. Soon I delivered a talk at our annual national Professional Convention for the AVH (Academy of Veterinary Homeopaths). Revisiting Dr. J Compton Burnett's book, Vaccinosis and It's Cure By Thuja, over a century later, I had rediscovered the link of vaccinations to ill health, dis eased states.

During the same period of time the Master's Program at Chi Institute was entered. I was one of the first to be awarded a Traditional Chinese Medical Practitioner Certification and Acupuncture, Chinese Herbal Therapy, Chinese Food Therapy and Tui-Na Ah Mo. I went to China to study TCVM in China and my degree was from South China University of Agriculture along with Chi Institute in Florida. I then was asked to author the chapter on treatment of cancer in small animals for the text book; Practical Guide to Traditional Chinese Veterinary Medicine. I had researched Chinese Medicine and found that they had entertained the possibility of benefits of vaccination to prevent disease, 500 years prior to Edward Jenning but determined the vaccine to not benefit the patient and abandoned vaccination.

I also attended a course at Healing Oasis under Dr. Pedro Rivera for veterinarians interested in learning advanced neurology and spinal manipulation, animal chiropractic. The different modalities that leant ability to address disease in my patients without drugs, without toxic chemicals was a path I wanted o continue down. At the time I was invited for a position at MIT, Massachusetts Institute of Technology, was the same time that I had made the connection to disease from vaccinations in the veterinary patients. Had I taken the position at MIT and studied Comparative Anatomy would I have still continued pursuing the link of vaccinations to dis ease?

Then I authored a book on Vaccinosis or the damage flowing being vaccinated. Over 700 victims of vaccine damage was witnessed within 3 months at a veterinary facility I worked at in Massachusetts. The clients received no nutritional information for how to feed their animals properly and the repeating of vaccinations continued every year with everything they could inject. I saw so many euthanasias every week, for animals with multiple autoimmune diseases and cancer, the average age to be put to death was 5-7 years of age. I began to document with laboratory reports, histopaths from pathologists that commended my work in the biopsy of cancers in the animals while looking for the aluminum blue grey foreign body that was associated with the vaccination. Pathologists continued to commend me in submitting blood samples for titers to the diseases rather than to just mindlessly repeat vaccinations.

Soon I was challenging anyone that tried to pretend that a vaccination, an abnormal immune assault was not the reasons just about any of our highly vaccinated animals were suffering Type I-IV hypersensitivity reactions, why autoimmune diseases and cancers were adverse events of vaccination. Like a few of my homeopathic colleagues I witnessed seeing the pathway of the aggressive vaccination protocols to the chronic disease state, the highly inflamed and unhealthy immune state. Soon my website became a magnet for adverse vaccine events as I was able to write, quite prolifically about what I was seeing. I wrote for Dogs Naturally, The New Zealand Journal of Natural Medicine, several other publications and a number of my colleagues' syndicated columns. Radio Shows and interviews and many webinars later, I found myself being asked to consult in legal cases on vaccine damage. Then along with Dr. Jean Dodds, I was sworn in to be a court certified expert to testify on veterinary vaccine damage.

Currently, I help clients all over the world, patients all over the world that are suffering the adverse effects of vaccination. I help them see the pathway to immune dys regulation that took place; I help them find ways to recovery using naturopathic medicine. I do not support vaccinations; I do not support unhealthy commercially processed foods. I do support us understanding how powerful our creator is that gave us such an awesome miraculous body. I stand now with my colleagues that also see that most everything we see in veterinary practice is the result of vaccination administration. No longer do I worry about the medical hubris that brought us to the situation; rather I am excited to help teach pathways to getting well, to getting healthier. I admit I didn't learn that in veterinary school, but I am happy to relay that I learned these things in our "other" doctor school.

Alternatives which should be the mainstream, that is my specialty and that is the kind of doctor I am, a healer, an educator. One who testifies for the truth and provides the evidence necessary to see where health and wellness comes from and to what dangerous medical practice act takes health away. I encourage my colleagues in Aescuplian Authority and to stand up for your patients, not for the selling of products that do not create health but rather the lifestyles that are life promoting. Be the kind of doctor your patients would want, one that protects the patient's interest first, not corporations and not an industry of good mates.

dr-jordan.com

NATURAL APPROACH TO TREATMENT AND PREVENTION OF
TICK PARALYSIS IN DOGS

Dr. Peter Dobias

How to keep ticks from attaching and spreading disease to your dog

Did you know ticks belong to the spider family? When you look closer, they indeed look like spiders with eight tiny legs and they also have an insatiable hunger for blood. Ticks are like the 'kamikaze' of spiders because they are much more daring than their bigger cousins. Instead of feeding on flies and other insects, they like to latch onto mammals and be carried miles away from their origin. They have evolved into stealthy biting machines, injecting anaesthetic into the bite to remain unnoticed.

1   Tick paralysis is one of the most dramatic and frightening conditions. One moment your dog is fine and a few hours later he or she may become completely paralyzed. If the condition is recognized and treated early, your dog will recover very fast. However, if you or your veterinarian fails to diagnose this problem correctly, the toxic paralyzing substance in tick saliva can, in the worst-case scenario, cause respiratory arrest and death.

2   This is why reading and sharing this article is so important.

3   This article includes information on the following:

- Cause of tick paralysis
- How does the tick toxin work
- Treatment of tick paralysis
- Natural methods of tick paralysis prevention

Cause of Tick Paralysis

Tick paralysis is caused by a salivary toxin that ticks release when they attach and feed on the host. There are different species of ticks that cause this condition and not every tick bite will cause paralysis.

The most toxic species, Ixodes Holocyclus, lives on the Eastern Coast of Australia, where the mortality of dogs with tick paralysis is around 10 percent.

The North American ticks transmitting tick paralysis are much less dangerous, however they should not be underestimated. The main species that causes tick paralysis in North America are Dermacentor andersoni (the Rocky Mountain wood tick) and Dermacentor variabilis, the American dog tick.

Tick paralysis often occurs in spring and early summer, but it can happen throughout tick season. Ticks are prevalent in certain regions, but they can be quickly transported to areas that have a low population. As a result, dog lovers and practitioners unused to seeing ticks and tick paralysis may misdiagnose the condition.

This is one of the reasons why I decided not to give you any maps or geographical locations of tick paralysis incidence. If you see ticks in your area, this condition is likely present and if you do not see ticks, the condition may be still present.

In some regions, ticks may also be active in the winter, but they usually stop feeding when the ground is frozen.

How does the toxin work?

The core principle of neurotoxin production is not clearly understood. There are some opinions that the toxin may be produced with the help of a microorganism residing in ticks.

What we do know is the toxin is released into the blood stream when ticks are engorged. The injected neurotoxin disturbs the exchange of electrolytes, such as calcium, sodium and potassium in the muscles cells. It also interrupts the connection between the nerves and muscles (the synapses), which leads to muscle paralysis.

What is fascinating and frightening is the level of development of ticks as a disease carrier. It is hard to believe such a small and insignificant creature can cause symptoms such as partial or complete leg paralysis and difficulty breathing and swallowing. This can sometimes lead to aspiration pneumonia (lung infection due to inhaling food or water).

Tick paralysis affects the nerve impulse transfer to the muscles, which leads to the inability of the muscles to contract, or paralysis. However, this condition does not affect the sensory nerves. In other words, your dog has skin and muscle sensation, however they cannot move their muscles.

Treatment of tick paralysis

- The most important part of tick paralysis is to remove all ticks. The most common locations are around the head and ears, but ticks can be pretty much anywhere. Examining your dog inch by inch with a fine comb and tons of patience is crucial and can be life-saving.

- You should start seeing improvement within 24 hours and a complete recovery in three days.

- When it comes to the most toxic tick, Ixodes Holocyclus in Eastern Australia, an injection of TAS antitoxin (similar to tetanus antitoxin) is the treatment of choice. Removing the tick itself will not always result in recovery.

- IV therapy, hospitalization, monitoring of urine output, breathing and body temperature is important. Because of the muscle paralysis, some animals may lose the ability to regulate temperature and may overheat or get cold.

- In some severe cases, a ventilator to support respiratory function is needed and the overall mortality of this condition is approximately five percent, even when the dog receives the proper treatment.

Supportive therapy consists of boosting the immune system with probiotics, plant-based minerals and green superfood and omega-3 oils, which are proven to have a strong anti-inflammatory effect.

Tick infestation and paralysis prevention

Many people are still unaware that conventional flea and tick products can be as equally harmful and dangerous as tick themselves. For more info, click here.

The other challenge is most conventional flea products don't prevent ticks attaching, which doesn't solve the issue of tick-borne diseases.

Ticks live in grassy areas and usually wait on a blade of grass and wait for the right opportunity to crawl on a host. Repelling and preventing ticks from attachment with natural tick products during the tick seasons (when the ground is not frozen) is an effective way to prevent tick paralysis and other tick borne diseases.

Finally, if you know you live in a tick-infested area, check your dog for ticks regularly to remove them as soon as possible.

http://peterdobias.com/

Healthy & long life for your dog, *naturally...*

'Enhancing the Life of *your* Greyhound'

Where - The Room in the Rodings, Dunmow Road, Beaucamp Roding, Essex, CM5 0PF

When - Sunday 1st October 2017 10:00 - 16:30

Join us on an educational day all about improving & enhancing the lives of retired racing greyhounds

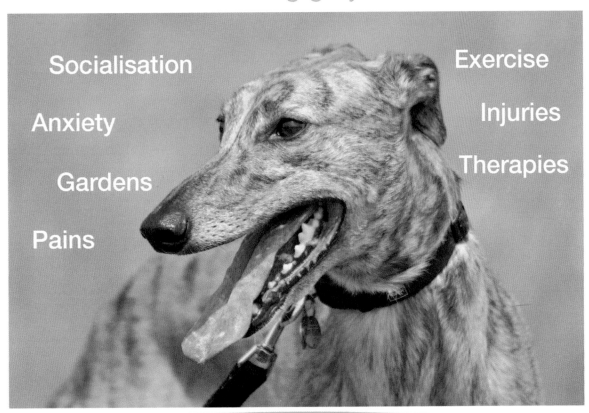

Socialisation

Exercise

Anxiety

Injuries

Gardens

Therapies

Pains

For more info contact Pennie on 07910 720961 or info@horseandhoundschool.co.uk

Held in support of the

Greyhound Trust

www.greyhoundtrust.org.uk

Registered Charity: 269668 & SCO44047

Canine Health Concern

Catherine O'Driscoll

PET WARNING:

Record numbers at risk of diseases as owners fail to vaccinate them… So went the heading in a June 21st edition of The Express.

"SIX MILLION pets are at risk of deadly diseases because owners failed to have them vaccinated when they were young, warns a hard hitting report," screamed the sub-heading.

The news item was the result, I presume, of a press release issued by the PDSA. Unfortunately, because the law doesn't require charities to confess who they're taking money from, we don't know whether a veterinary vaccine manufacturer offered the organisation its 40 pieces of silver.

The article went on to say: "In 2011, 82 per cent of dogs and 72 per cent of cats received primary vaccination courses, but last year this had declined to 75 per cent (7 million dogs) and 65 per cent (6.7 million) cats, respectively. "What will shock many conscientious pet owners is the large number of people who are not getting their animals protected from illnesses.

"The report highlights how 14 per cent of dog owners, 22 per cent of cat owners and a third of those with rabbits said vaccinations were not necessary, using excuses such as their pets do not mix with other animals.

"Commenting on findings the PDSA describes as 'troubling', its head of pet health and welfare Nicola Martin said: 'The decreasing number of dogs, cats and rabbits receiving vaccinations is a great concern for the health and welfare of the nation's pets.'"

Well if the PDSA had asked me to take part in their survey, I wouldn't have told them that I don't vaccinate because I can't afford vaccines, or that my dogs don't mix with other animals. I'd have told them that since I stopped vaccinating my dogs 25 years ago, I've had the absolute joy of living with totally vaccine-free dogs – which means that rather than taking my sickly dogs to the vet every other week, they have cause to go to the vet every five years or so (except for poor Freddie who has inherited thyroid disease and a heart murmur).

But, actually, these figures might be a worry, since I wouldn't recommend anyone who feeds commercial pet 'food' to leave their dogs unprotected from the diseases many of us don't vaccinate against. Nutrition – as you know – is Nature's defence against pathogens. Our dogs need to eat real food if we're not going to vaccinate them.

They would also benefit from natural immune-boosters such as Transfer Factor, nosodes, and any of the many anti-viral and antibiotic herbs.

Of course the PDSA doesn't seem to have spoken to anyone in the greatly expanding natural rearing movement. Or maybe what we know doesn't fit their ideology or funding requirements.

Unfortunately charities don't have to make funding sources visible, so we don't know if the veterinary vaccine industry is behind the press release. And where are these outbreaks they're warning us about?

Proof: vaccines are contaminated with glyphosate

From NaturalNews.com

Scientists Anthony Samsel and Stephanie Seneff, who recently published their fifth peer-reviewed paper on the herbicide glyphosate's contributions to disease, are on the verge of publishing a sixth – which promises to be even more explosive than their prior works.

Backed by strong supporting data from multiple labs, Samsel and Seneff say that many popular vaccines are contaminated with glyphosate used in the weedkiller Roundup, and could initiate a disastrous "cascade of disease" when injected.

The World Health Organization admits that glyphosate is 'probably carcinogenic in humans' and many scientists (and holistic health experts) say that glyphosate is already linked with diseases such as autism, inflammatory bowel disease and non-Hodgkin's lymphoma – to name only a few.

Why are vaccines loaded with glyphosate?

Vaccine manufacturers use animal byproducts – such as egg protein, casein or gelatin – as a substrate to grow the vaccine, and in some cases these animal products are used as a stabiliser in the actual vaccine.

If the animals are sourced from factory farms, the odds are good that they've been consuming feed that not only contains GMOs but has been sprayed with glyphosate – resulting in injections of the toxin directly into people's bodies, or into the bodies of animals they will consume.

In addition, Samsel points out that gelatin is already an ingredient in many popular consumer products, including vitamins, protein powders, beer, wine and other items.

Samsel notes that he thought his chances of finding glyphosate in some vaccines were "pretty good," but even he seems shocked at the extent of the contamination.

FLEAS ON DOGS AND CATS

W Jean Dodds

If your companion pet has the MDR-1 Mutation, epilepsy or is prone to seizures, this animal should avoid flea preventatives that contain the chemicals, spinosad, or any of the isoxazolines.

Further, using flea preventatives should be reserved for situations where there is a highly likelihood of exposure or you know for certain your companion pet is prone to fleas or has fleas.

Generally, you will have to go through a flea season

or two to ascertain your pet's vulnerability to fleas and to any side effects of using chemical flea preventives.

Some veterinarians suggest a dietary change to a more nourishing food – particularly one that is grain-free. One highly-touted rationale is that fleas are attracted to high blood sugar levels just like mosquitoes. But, first and foremost, fleas and mosquitoes are not the same insect.

Best Health Article 2016

Janet McAllister, Ph.D., an entomologist in the Division of Vector-Born Diseases at the Centers for Disease Control and Prevention states that higher blood glucose levels do not attract mosquitoes.

From experience, however, we know that the attraction of mosquitoes to one person over another is quite variable and can differ between the various mosquito species. Observed instances include the output of carbon dioxide, people who metabolize cholesterol quickly, certain bodily bacteria, and even exercise-induced lactic acid release.

Needless to say, this is not meant to discourage you from feeding your companion pet a healthier diet. The point is that scientific studies have not proven that increased blood glucose concentration attracts fleas.

One has to remember that immunity is complex and affected by variables such as genetics, food, diseases and environment. If a dietary change helps prevent flea load on a pet, it could be correlated to a reduced sensitivity to a food because the immune system is less compromised.

My most significant personal flea experience involved two English Pointers that I bred. Cameo was orange and white with a pink nose and toenails, whereas her sister, Winnie, was black and white with a black nose and toenails. At the time, I lived near the beach and Cameo would return covered in fleas. Winnie, by contrast, might only get one or two, but they would soon jump off her onto Cameo. They ate the same food and slept on the same bed.

So why did Cameo attract the fleas?

It is well-known that skin pH in humans differs along the pigmentation spectrum. The same rings true for dogs and cats. Pets with lighter skin and haircoat, like Cameo's, generally have heightened sensitivities to immunological challenges and environmental exposures.

So, yes; I believe a correlation exists between the attraction for fleas, and bodily metabolic health and immune tolerance responses.

Do we know the exact correlation?

No.

The best preventive aid is to promote health with optimal nutrition, weight control, reduced stress and appropriate exercise. These factors will contribute to a more balanced immune system and potentially help reduce or eliminate flea (and other parasite) burdens.

CHC note: raw feeders do notice that their dogs are less attractive to fleas.

Alfred Plechner DVM, in his book, Pet Allergies, remedies for an epidemic, claimed that dogs given vitamin and mineral supplements were virtually flea-proof – so maybe it's not about blood sugar levels, but nutrient levels?

We don't recommend ANY chemical flea control products; we've never heard of one which doesn't have some level of harm.

If your dogs have fleas, bear in mind that 95% of them will be in your house and not on your dog. Therefore the only way to get rid of fleas is to treat the house. Diatomaceous Earth can be sprinkled around the house, making sure you get all the corners and edges (such as carpet edges, beds, and so on). Then vacuum up. At the same time, you can use DE, neem and essential oils to make your dogs less attractive to the little suckers. Adding a vitamin and mineral mix such as Spirulina to their food, as well as garlic, should do the trick.

MSG In Dog Food Can Cause Brain Damage

When I found myself suffering from intermittent insomnia, I felt sure it was related to digestion. I'd be fast asleep and then suddenly wake up feeling very agitated, yet there was absolutely nothing worrying me. I traced this back to having eaten MSG.

The worst night was after a weekend workshop when I'd really have appreciated some shut eye; the host had treated us all to a Chinese takeaway. Staying in her house, I ended up sitting in the car all night wishing I could sleep.

But MSG is also found in many processed foods – which I personally have good reason to avoid. Do you?

This article from Dogs Naturally magazine sums MSG up.

You're probably familiar with monosodium glutamate (MSG) as a flavour enhancer in Chinese restaurant food and a lot of packaged food products like canned soups and vegetables, processed meats, snacks like potato chips, salad dressings and frozen dinners.

The US Food and Drug Administration (FDA) classifies it as GRAS (Generally Recognized As Safe) but still, quite a lot of people experience unpleasant symptoms like headaches, flushing, sweating, nausea, heart palpitations, chest pain and facial numbness or tingling after eating food with MSG in it. If you're one of the people who doesn't feel good after eating anything with MSG in it, you may try to avoid it in your own food. But what about your dog?

MSG lurks in many pet foods as well. And your dog can't tell you he has a headache after eating it. MSG Alters Brain Response MSG is used as a flavour enhancer ... but it's actually quite tasteless itself.

It works by tricking the brain into thinking food tastes good. It's a type of neurotransmitter known as an excitotoxin, meaning it overstimulates the brain, causing an overproduction of dopamine. This creates a brief sensation of wellbeing. But it damages the brain and alters its ability to respond to the signal from the hormone leptin that tells us we're full ... which is why, when you eat foods containing MSG, you just want to keep eating, making the food seem almost addictive.

Of course, when it comes to dogs, most of them are greedy and just want to keep eating anyway ... but if your dog's eating kibble, MSG in his food might be increasing his seemingly endless hunger!

How It Can Harm Your Dog

It's scary to think that MSG might damage your dog's brain. Dr Russell Blaylock, author of "Excitotoxins: The Taste that Kills" says that it can cause brain damage (in humans) and may trigger or aggravate learning disabilities as well as diseases like Alzheimer's, Parkinson's, and Lou Gehrig's. But that's not all. Studies have shown other potential risks. A study in the 2008 Journal of Autoimmunity showed that injecting MSG into mice led to liver inflammation, along with obesity and Type 2 diabetes. And what's worse, the effects accumulate over time.

How To Avoid MSG

That's easier said than done. It's really hard to find MSG on food labels. The FDA allows more than 40 ingredients that contain it. But because it isn't added directly to the food, it doesn't have to be listed on the label. One of the pet food industry's favourite forms of MSG is hydrolysed protein, also used to enhance flavour. If you see "natural flavouring" or "digest" on the label, it's probably hydrolysed protein. Apart from natural flavour, it can also appear under other names, including:

- Any type of protein isolate (e.g. soy protein isolate)
- Any type of textured protein (such as textured vegetable protein)
- Autolyzed yeast
- Hydrolysed yeast
- Yeast extracts or yeast nutrient or yeast food
- Soy extracts

- Soy concentrate
- Sodium caseinate or calcium caseinate
- Disodium inosinate or disodium guanylate (which are flavour enhancers effective only in the presence of MSG)
- MSG (monosodium glutamate)
- Monopotassium glutamate
- Glutamate, glutamic acid, or free glutamate

Even if you're a careful label reader, there are other ways your dog may be getting MSG in his diet. There's a product called AuxiGro that contains hydrolyzed proteins and monosodium glutamate. AuxiGro is used to increase crop yields and is sprayed on crops like lettuce (various types), broccoli, tomatoes, potatoes, peanuts, celery, cucumbers, navy and pinto beans; grapes; onions; bell, green and jalapeño peppers, strawberries and watermelons. When vegetables and fruit start to spoil, they're often used in pet foods and advertised as all natural healthy ingredients. There's no way of knowing whether MSG is in the produce in dog foods. Processed free glutamic acid is in many dairy products like milk or cottage cheese, so if you add dairy to your dog's diet, he may be getting some MSG that way too.

If your dog's a poop eater and you give him one of the products intended to prevent this behaviour, beware ... most of them contain some form of MSG, listed as monosodium glutamate, glutamic acid, or one of the other alternative names listed above. By the way, just about all of these products contain other undesirable chemical ingredients as well, so you might want to find another way to stop your dog's poop eating habit. Dogsnaturallymagazine.com

www.canine-health-concern.org.uk

NICK THOMPSON

CANINE NUTRITION

Hypothyroidism & Vaccinations

brought to you by

holisticvet

RAW DOG FOOD

WWW.RAWDOGFOOD.CO/SEMINARS

We are thrilled to be able to bring you this new video series by the incredible Nick Thompson: **Canine Nutrition, Hypothyroidism and Vaccinations** features over five hours worth of video covering the following subjects:

An introduction to Raw Food for Dogs:

Why consider changing from tins or kibble?

- How safe and complete are raw foods?
- How to choose a ready made raw food
- How to make your own raw food diet

Hypothyroidism, Behaviour, Epilepsy & Chronic Disease:

- 43% of English Setters have Autoimmune Thyroiditis
- Golden Retriever, Cocker Spaniel, Boxer and Labrador breeds are all in the top 25 most commonly affected breeds
- Groups at higher risk for behavioural disorders due to thyroid disease include: pedigrees, neutered males and females and mid to large sized dogs

Vaccination in the 21st Century:

- Why "re-starting" vaccines is "inconsistent" with the principles of immunological memory
- Why blood testing (titre testing) is the future
- When to titre test
- When to vaccinate puppies; when not to
- When to vaccinate old dogs; when not to
- How useful is Kennel Cough Vaccine

We think this is a complete bargain at only **£24.99,**

Click **here** for access or go to http://t.co/WvKTa1WUGt

Recommended Reading

Canine Nutrigenomics	Dodds, J.W. & Laverdure, D.R
Food Pets Die For	Ann N. Martin
Heal Your Dog the Natural Way	Richard Allport
Natural Healthcare for Pets	Richard Allport
Paleo Dog	Jean Hofve & Celeste Yarnall
Pottenger's Cats	Francis M. Pottenger
Raw Meaty Bones	Tom Lonsdale
Shock to the System	Catherine O'Driscoll
Ten Top Tips on Reducing the Cost of Raw Feeding	H B Turner
The BARF Diet	Dr Ian Billinghurst
The Complete Herbal Handbook for the Dog and Cat	Juliette de Baïracli Levy
The Healthful Dog Blog	H B Turner
The Homeopathic Treatment of Small Animals	Christopher Day
The Natural Rearing Breeder	H B Turner
The Science Behind Canine Raw Feeding	H B Turner
The Science of Homoeopathy	George Vithoulkas
Unlock Your Dog's Potential	Sarah Fisher
What Vets Don't Tell you about Vaccines	Catherine O'Driscoll

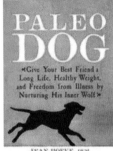

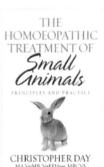

Recommended Resources

Amazon	www.amazon.co.uk/.com
American Homeopathic Veterinary Medical Association	www.ahvma.org
Association of Non-Veterinary Natural Animal Health Practitioners	www.annahp.co.uk
Australian Association of Holistic Veterinarians	www.aha.com.au
British Association of Homeopathic Veterinary Surgeons	www.bahvs.com
Canine Health Concern (CHC)	www.canine-health-concern.org.uk
Chip Me Not	www.ChipMeNot.org
Complementary Veterinary Medicine Group of the South African Veterinary Association	www.cvmg.co.za
DEFRA	www.defra.gov.uk
Merck Veterinary Manual	www.merckmanuals.com/vet
Price Pottenger Nutrition Foundation (PPNF)	www.ppnf.org
Raw Food Vets	www.rawfoodvets.com
Royal College of Veterinary Surgeons	www.rcvs.org.uk
VacciCheck Vets	www.petwelfarealliance.org/vaccicheck.html
Veterinary Medical Directorate	www.vmd.defra.gov.uk
Worm Count Lab	www.wormcount.com
World Small Animal Veterinary Association	www.WSAVA.org

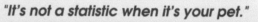

"It's not a statistic when it's your pet."

Healthful Dog Journalzine is sponsored by ANNAHP and Wagdale & published by Talen Publications

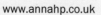

www.annahp.co.uk   www.wagdale.org.uk   facebook.com/TalenPublications

Printed in Great Britain
by Amazon